THE LIFE OF
ST. BRIGID
OF KILDARE
by cogitosus

and other selected writings

THE LIFE OF
ST · BRIGID
OF KILDARE
by cogitosus

and other selected writings

CRUACHAN
HILL PRESS

ISBN: 978-1-957206-07-3
Cover Art by Jessica Fellmeth

cRuachan
HiLL PReSS

Published by
Cruachan Hill Press
12552 E Michigan Ave.
Grass Lake, MI 49240
www.cruachanhill.com

Printed and Bound in the United States of America

Dedication and Acknowledgement

Thanks to Jesse Griffiths for her editing work, Jessica Fellmeth for her beautiful cover, and Marcella of *Trias Thaumaturga* for the excellent resources. This book is dedicated to all who love the saints of Ireland.

Table of Contents

Introduction
"Brigid, Excellent Woman"

ince the late Middle Ages at least, it has become custom to lump St. Brigid of Kildare, St. Patrick, and St. Columba together as the three great saints of Ireland. In 1571, the great Jesuit saint, Edmund Campion, wrote of the triple burial of the three saints Downpatrick, saying, "in sainct Patrickes tyme floreshid St. Bryde the vrygyn and St. Colme in Don, where there bodys sone after the conquest and also saynct Patrickes body were fonde." Around the same time Richard Stalinhurst, Anglo-Irish poet, composed this charming couplet expressing the same sentiment:

> Three bodies lie buried in Down's hill,
> Patrick, Brigid, and Colmcille

It seemed the three were inseparable. Thomas Messingham's 1624 Latin hagiographical work, *Florilegium insulae sanctorum seu vitae et acta sanctorum Hiberniae* ("Anthology of the Island of the Saints, or The Lives and Acts of the Saints of Ireland"), had for its frontispiece an engraving of these saints standing in three alcoves representing the three glories of the Irish Church.

This picture would be reused again in 1874 to adorn Fr. James O'Leary's work *The Most Ancient Lives of St. Patrick*. The following year, the controversial Irish nationalist nun, Sister Mary Francis Cusack, published a work called *Trias Thaumaturga*, or "Three Wonderworking Saints of Ireland: St. Patrick, St. Bridget, and St. Columba." Even St. Columba himself seemed to have a supernatural premonition that he belonged with Patrick and Brigid; before he died, he supposedly prophesied his entombment with the others—

> My prosperity in guiltless Hy (i.e., Iona)
> And my soul in Derry
> And my body under the flag
> Beneath which are Patrick and Brigid[1]

Eventually this triad came to be regarded as the patron saints of Ireland, especially during the Irish War of Independence (1919-1921) when Ireland's ancient saints became powerful symbols of national unity. Earlier this year, Cruachan Hill Press released a revised edition of the *Life of St. Columba* as told by St. Adomnán. Now, we turn to the second member of the triad, the famous St. Brigid.

St. Brigid has always had a popular following in Ireland, but, like Columba, has struggled to step out from under the shadow of the great St. Patrick. Fortunately, a new era of interest in Brigid's life seems to be dawning. The past thirty years has seen several new translations of Cogitosus's *Life of St. Brigid the Virgin,* as well as a proliferation of scholarly articles on the great foundress of Kildare. There is also a considerable amount

---

[1] Mary Francis Cusack, *An Illustrated History of Ireland,* Chapter IX, "Shrines of the Three Saints" (Longmans, Green & Co.: London, 1868)

of popular interest in Brigid. In wake of a groundswell of popular support, in 2022 the government of Ireland declared St. Brigid's Day (February 1) a national holiday.[2]

Neo-pagans, too, have adopted St. Brigid as an emblem of their movement. Skeptics have long nurtured a suspicion that the historical St. Brigid never existed—that she is a Christianized version of an ancient Celtic goddess. Proponents of this theory generally point to the curious concurrence of Brigid's feast day with the Celtic festival of Imbolc, as well as some stories in the *vitae* of Brigid that supposedly correspond with pagan folklore. They see her as an exemplification of their post-modern values: feminism, ecological activism, tolerance, and an eclectic pantheistic spirituality. Of course, nothing we read in any Brigittine literature suggests that St. Brigid would have condoned these ideals. Historical considerations are ultimately irrelevant, however, as neo-pagans derive far more value from Brigid as a symbol than an historical figure.

Brigid is not the only Irish Catholic saint to be transmuted into a neo-pagan icon. Indeed, modernity has witnessed the entire cultural edifice of Irish Christianity subject to kind of paganization. A brief perusal of the "Celtic Spirituality" section of any religious bookstore will tell you all you need to know about how modernity has reimagined Irish Christianity. You will not find books about Jesus Christ, the Catholic Church, or Christian holiness, but about relaxation techniques, the Irish spirit wheel, "oneness with nature," and meditative breathing exercises. It is heavily syncretized, often retaining Christian iconography only as Jungian archetypes while the underlying

---

[2] By comparison, St, Patrick's Day has been a national holiday in Ireland since 1903.

structure is thoroughly pagan. One scholarly article attempting to explain this belief system from a sociological standpoint observes that "contemporary Celtic spirituality routinely and syncretically blends Christian and Pagan elements of ideology." [3] The same author goes on to say that Celtic spirituality, as it is understood today

> ...encompasses practices, beliefs, attitudes, and values that are loosely based on themes and remnants of Ancient Celtic traditions that survive in fairy tales and Celtic mythology... contemporary Celtic spiritual practices [are] widely regarded as embodying less authoritative, organized, institutional, and dogmatic phenomena than is generally implied by the term "religion." [4]

This description gets to the heart of why this bastardized version of Celtic Christianity is so popular—it affords its adherents the opportunity to embrace what they consider an authentically western spirituality that is not tied to any dogma, institution, creed, or hierarchy. It retains the aesthetically pleasing aspects of Christianity without the creeds of the Church, offering a spirituality where the only criterion of truth is the subjective experience of the individual. In other words, it represents a Christianity shorn of its traditional strictures—Christianity as progressives wish all Christianity would become.

---

[3] M.J. Drake Spaeth, "Celtic Spirituality," in *Encyclopedia of Psychology and Religion*, ed. D.A. Leeming (Springer: Boston, MA. 2014), pp. 291
[4] Ibid.

Cruachan Hill Press's publication of this little book on St. Brigid is an answer to this movement. It is an attempt to connect with, not an imagined Brigid the feminist or Brigid the ecologist, but Brigid the *saint*. Brigid was first and foremost a Catholic nun, and any presentation of her life and ideals that minimizes this fact not only does a disservice to Brigid's legacy but is positively destructive in its deception (readers interested in the question of Brigid's alleged connection to a pagan goddess will find the appendix essay on the historical merits of this theory to be of great value).

Let us, therefore, begin to undo the paganized knot our contemporaries have wound about St. Brigid by going back to her life as told in the ancient sources.

Sources on the Life of Saint Brigid

Most scholars place the death of St. Brigid around 525. The earliest accounts of her life come from two hymns written at least two generations after her death. The first is known as "Ultan's Hymn" on account of its author, St. Ultan of Ardbraccan (d. 657), Bishop of Ardbraccan (County Meath), abbot, and founder of a monastic school, among whose pupils was the famous Tírechán, biographer of St. Patrick. "Ultan's Hymn" is a brief, laudatory hymn praising the virtues and powers of St. Brigid. Its opening line is perhaps the most famous in Brigittine lore, calling her "excellent woman, a flame golden." In fact, the Gaelic title of the hymn in *Brigit Bé Bithmaith*, "Brigit, Excellent Woman." St. Ultan invokes her against demons and illness and calls her "one of the pillars of the kingdom, with Patrick the pre-eminent." Even from the very beginning, Brigid was associated with the great Patrick as a foundation stone of Irish Christianity.

"Ultan's Hymn" does not contain any biographical information about Brigid, beyond calling her "saint of the *Laighin*," that is, the people of Leinster, as Kildare was located within the ancient Kingdom of Leinster. Ultan did, however, reputedly collect a substantial amount of information about the life of the saint, which he entrusted to his disciple, St. Broccán (d. 650). St. Broccán used this information to compose a much longer work, "Broccán's Hymn." Comprised of 53 stanzas, "Broccán's Hymn" is a metrical life of St. Brigid. The first few stanzas are dedicated to praising her virtues; the remainder recount various miracles for which she was renowned, many of which also appear in the later *vita* of Cogitosus. Beyond the miracle stories, there is little by way of biographical information in "Broccán's Hymn"; he tells us neither where Brigid was born, nor how she came to religious life. "Broccán's Hymn" is interested only in her supernatural virtues and works. Both "Ultan's Hymn" and "Broccán's Hymn" can be found in their entirety in this book.

Two prose lives of St. Brigid were written in the 7th century as well. These are typically lumped together and known as *Vita Sanctae Brigitae* I and II. *Vita I* is believed to have been written by St. Ailerán (d. 665), a learned scholar of St. Finnian's School of Clonard.[5] *Vita II* was written by Cogitosus, a monk of Kildare, around 650. For generations, scholars have gone round about whether *Vita I* or *Vita II* was written first. Today, there seems to be a consensus that Cogitosus's *Vita II* was the earlier of the

---

[5] Although a minority opinion considers it may have been written by St. Ultan.

two. Those who wish to read a scholarly argument to this effect should consult the essay "Cogitosus's Life of St. Brigit: Content and Value," published in Volume 117 of the *The Journal of the Royal Society of Antiquaries of Ireland* in 1987 by Sean Connolly and Jean-Michael Picard, two researchers who have made a contemporary English translation of *Vita II.*

Sadly, there appears to be no accessible English translations of St. Ailerán's *Vita I*, at least that this editor is aware of. Nevertheless, the content of *Vita I* was reproduced almost in its entirety in a medieval homily on the life of Brigid from a text called the *Leabhar Breac.* The *Leabhar Breac* ("The Speckled Book") is an early 14th century manuscript containing a collection of Hiberno-Latin and Middle Irish writings. Its contents are eclectic, including the lives of Sts. Patrick, Columba, Cellach, and Martin; the "Martyrology of Óengus", the *Rule of the Céli Dé*, a Marian litany, the apocryphal *Gospel of Nicodemus*, and other oddities, such as histories of Philip of Macedon and Alexander the Great. It is among this collection that we find a life of St. Brigid. The *Leabhar Breac's* biography of Brigid appears to be a close paraphrase of Ailerán's *Vita I.* Though the *Leabhar Breac* calls it a "homily," it resembles a *vita* much more than a homily.

The account of Brigid's life from the *Leabhar Breac* fills in the biographical details missing from the writings of Ultan, Broccán, and Cogitosus. We learn of her parents, her mother's upbringing as a slave, and Brigid's own rearing in the house of a druid (whom the text calls a "wizard"). We also learn of Brigid's entrance into religious life, her ecclesiastical acquaintances, and some of her miraculous works. It speaks briefly of her establishment of Kildare, gives us a sketch of her personal habits, and ends with the account of her holy death and Viaticum given by St. Ninnid.

Vita II is *The Life of St. Brigid the Virgin* by Cogitosus. Unlike St. Ailerán, Cogitosus was a monk of Kildare, Brigid's own monastery. Like any loyal religious, Cogitosus had an obligation to promote the cultus of his monastic founder. *Vita II* is thus more of a conventional hagiography, focusing almost exclusively on the miracles of St. Brigid. It is from Cogitosus's account that we get the most famous tales of Brigid, like her hanging her clothes on a sunbeam or milking a cow three times in a single day. Historically, Cogitosus's *Vita II* is valuable for its lavish description of the tombs of Sts. Brigid and Conleth and the church of Kildare as it appeared in the mid-7th century when it had already become a vibrant pilgrim destination. It is the most detailed extant description of a major Irish church from the golden age of Irish Catholicism.

Modern commentators have remarked on Cogitosus's strange omission of any substantial biographical details about Brigid's life in his *Vita II*. Besides the names of her parents, he tells us little else of her background. Since Kildare was the site of Brigid's tomb and the center of her cultus, presumably Cogitosus would have access to reliable information about Brigid's life; indeed, he states that in his day there was an "extensive tradition" of Brigittine lore he knew of. We do not know how long Cogitosus lived, but assuming he was at least middle aged when he wrote *Vita II* around 650, it was certainly possible that he could have spoken with elderly persons who had known St. Brigid in their youth. If he had access to all these living and documentary traditions, why, then, does *Vita II* omit any discussion of Brigid's biography?

One possible explanation is that Cogitosus did not wish to draw attention to Brigid's servile origins. *Vita I* makes it clear that Brigid's mother was not only a slave but a concubine. Brigid was raised by a druid, if not as a slave herself, then at least in semi-free status. Though such arrangements were common and not considered scandalous during Brigid's youth (the middle 5th century, when Ireland was still deeply pagan), by Cogitosus's time Christianity had grown considerably, such that there was a stigma attached to the servitude and concubinage of Brigid's mother and, to a lesser degree, Brigid herself. As a monk of Kildare, Cogitosus was eager to promote the cultus of Brigid and draw pilgrims to her tomb. He was therefore solicitous to omit biographical details that might have been considered unflattering. St. Ailerán, meanwhile, was not of Kildare but Clonard, not only from a different monastic establishment but from an entirely different kingdom: Kildare is in County Leinster in the Irish Midlands, whereas Clonard was further north, in County Meath, which in those days was a completely different kingdom. Though St. Ailerán clearly had a deep devotion to St. Brigid and respect for her life, he was neither of her monastery nor her people, and thus did not feel as constrained in his choice of content as Cogitosus may have. This is admittedly only a theory, but a plausible theory, and one held by more than a few experts of Brigittine lore.

The astute reader will notice that Ultan, Broccán, Ailerán, and Cogitosus were all contemporaries of one another. That these hymns and *vitae* should all be composed within such a small window is astonishing. The generation from 630-660 must have been an extraordinary period of growth for the cultus of St. Brigid. The conversion of Ireland begun by Sts. Palladius and Patrick in the 5th century had accelerated to the point that pilgrimage was becoming common. We can imagine a groundswell of popular interest in Brigid, fueled by the ambitions of the Leinster kings of the Uí Dúnlainge dynasty, Fáelán mac Colmáin (636-666) and Fiannamail mac Máele Tuile (666-680), who were no doubt eager to bolster the reputation of Kildare through their royal patronage. These texts were no doubt written to answer the growing demand for information about the marvelous saint of Kildare. From across span of thirteen centuries, we can still sense the pride and excitement in Cogitosus's voice when he writes of the bustling center of Kildare in his own day:

> But who could convey in words the supreme beauty of her church and the countless wonders of her city, of which we would speak?...And who could number the varied crowds and countless people who gather in from all territories? Some come for the abundance of festivals; others come to watch the crowds go by; others come with great gifts to the celebration of the birth into heaven of St. Brigid.

There were several more lives of Brigid written in the first millennium: an anonymous life in Old Irish called the *Bethu Brigte* which dates from Carolingian times, a hexameter Latin poem composed by St. Colman around 800, and a *Vita III*, attributed sometimes to St. Donatus, sometimes to St. Coelan of Inishcaltra, dated sometime between 700-800. These, however, are based on the earlier works of the 7th century. The principal contributions to our knowledge of Brigid's historical life come from our four 7th century authors.

Brigid's Life

It is from the *Leabhar Breac*/Ailerán that we learn that Brigid's
father was Dubthach, a local ruler. The text infers that
Dubthach was a king, as his wife, Brechtnat, is called a queen.
The word "king" is extremely vague in Old Irish, however,
denoting a great variety of authority figures, from a *rí coiced*
(provincial king) right on down to a *rí tuaithe* (a petty chieftain
governing a confederation of families in a specified region).
Dubthach was likely among the latter.

Brigid's mother was Broicsech, a slave purchased by
Dubthach as a concubine. Dubthach's affection for Broicsech
bred resentment from Brechtnat. The situation was made
worse when Broicsech conceived. Dubthach, finding no peace
in his house due to the envy of Brechtnat, reluctantly sought
to sell Broicsech. Brigid's mother was sold or traded among
multiple men and gave birth to Brigid while working as a milk
woman for a druid ("wizard") named Maithgen, who had
leased her to a friend. In the sale of Brigid's mother to
Maithgen the druid, Dubthach had agreed to sell only
Broicsech, but stipulated that he wished to retain rights over
Brigid. After her birth, Brigid was reared in the household of
Maithgen as his ward with the understanding that Dubthach
retained a legal claim on her. Brigid was thus not a slave but
neither wholly free. This is not surprising, as ancient Ireland
had varying degrees of servitude. Brigid was likely of a legal
caste known as the "half-free," individuals who had personal
freedom but were accountable to a lord who had legal
responsibility for them. Her mother Broicsech, meanwhile,
remained bound in slavery, laboring and presumably being
used sexually by a variety of owners.

The precise religious observance of Brigid's family is uncertain. On the one hand, the *vitae* of Brigid imply that she was a Christian from youth; Cogitosus says her parents were both Christians. Furthermore, her father Dubthach was on familiar terms with the Bishops Mél and Melchu, hosting them at his home. This would suggest Brigid was born into a pious Christian household with strong connections to the local church.[6] On the other hand, Dubthach was clearly polygamous, the core drama of Brigid's early live being the rivalry between his two wives, Brechtnat and the concubine Broicsech. He also had no scruple about allowing his daughter to be raised by the druids, the pagan nemeses of the Christian priesthood. We may have difficulty reconciling such things with any sincere Christianity.

The likeliest explanation is that Brigid came from a nominally Christian family, but in a time when social values were in a state of flux. We know that elsewhere in Europe it took some time for pagan mores to yield to the ethics of the new faith; polygamy was still being practiced by the Franks in Charlemagne's time, almost three centuries after the conversion of Clovis. We can assume a similar state of affairs in 5th-6th century Ireland, when the Christian faith had a strong foothold but was far from dominant. Nor should we be surprised at the apparently congenial relationship evidenced between Christians and druids seen throughout the lives of Brigid. Other early Irish hagiographies paint a similar picture;

---

[6] There is a story in the *Leabhar Breac* about a "baptism" of Brigid witnessed by Maithgen the druid, but this appears to be a vision, as it is administered by angels. There is also no mentioned of water, only oil. The implication is not sacramental baptism, but of an supernatural anointing to serve God.

in Adomnán's *Life of St. Columba*, we see the saint conversing pleasantly with a druid over the details of a voyage, suggesting the saint and the druid were friends. [7] Though there was certainly a rivalry between the druids and the Christian monks, there must have also been a grudging respect among them as the two educated classes of Ireland. The druids were not merely the magicians we are familiar with from the stories of St. Patrick; they were poets, philosophers, and the keepers of Gaelic lore. The druids in the *Leabhar Breac* are not villains; on the contrary, they are witnesses to the power of God. The druid Maithgen accurately prophesies to Dubthach that the children of his wife Brechtnat will serve Brigid. Brigid was given her name by three angels who appeared before her birth, not to her Christian father, but to a pagan druid. Though pagan, the druids occasionally manifested supernatural gifts to accurately foretell the works of God.

Brigid began to demonstrate miraculous gifts as a girl, working miracles while in the household of the druid Maithgen. When she came of age, she returned to the house of Dubthach. Several of the miracles from the *Vita II* of Cogitosus relate to her life at home. The relationship between Brigid and her faither appears to have been strained; the *Leabhar Breac* tells us she frequently gave away his food and possessions without his permission, having recourse to God to make up the difference. She also desired to see her birth mother but was refused permission by Dubthach. Brigid, however, disobeyed her father and returned to the house of Maithgen to visit her mother, who was still enslaved. We are told that while there she worked a miracle by the multiplication of butter. Through this miracle

---

[7] See *Life of St. Columba*, Book II:34-35

she obtained the conversion of the druid and the freedom of her mother from bondage.

Brigid returned to Dubthach's house with her birth mother, which heightened tensions in the household. The text tells us her father was so wroth with her for this (and for giving away all his goods to the poor) that he decided to sell her into slavery. He accordingly took Brigid to the court of the Dunlang MacEnda, King of Leinster, to sell her. King Dunlag, however, recognized Brigid's virtue. He bought her from Dubthach for the price of an ivory handled sword and then straight away granted her freedom.

Her father immediately tried to yoke Brigid in marriage to a young nobleman. She refused, prompting insults from one of her stepbrothers, Beccan (the 9th century *Bethu Brigte* states that the reason her step-brothers were wroth was that her refusal deprived the family of the bride-price they had been counting on). After a particularly gruesome miracle involving Beccan's eyes exploding in their sockets, Dubthach gave up opposing Brigid and yielded his consent for her to take the veil.

Brigid was professed by the hand of St. Mél, Bishop of Ardagh and nephew of St. Patrick. Multiple versions of Brigid's life record that when giving the veil, St. Mél inadvertently read the order for episcopal consecration. More will be said on this when we discuss Brigid's legacy.

Both St. Aileran's *Vita I* and the *Bethu Brigte* affirm that Brigid attended a synod convened by St. Patrick at Tailtin. Modern commentators are quick to discount this as legend because of the chronological impossibility of Brigid and Patrick's lives overlapping here: Patrick is reckoned to have died in 461, and Brigid was not born until 451, meaning Brigid was never older than ten while St. Patrick was alive. Assuming

Brigid did not take the veil until she was at least seventeen or eighteen, she simply could not have seen Patrick at the time the Synod of Tailtin was convened; he would have been dead for at least a decade, probably longer. It must be remembered, however, that 461 is only one of two proposed dates for the death of Patrick. There is also a "late Patrick" tradition, which places his death in 493. This is, in fact, the traditional date, the earlier date being a modern revision. If 493 is the correct dating for Patrick's death, there is no reason Brigid could not have conversed with him at the Synod of Taitlin, as her life would have overlapped St. Patrick's by 42 years. Other Irish hagiographical traditions strongly affirm the friendship of Patrick and Brigid as well; the 9th century *Book of Armagh*, for example, says, "Between St. Patrick and St. Brigid, the pillars of the Irish people, there was so great a friendship of charity that they had but one heart and one mind. Through him and through her Christ performed many great works." The accounts of her acquaintance with St. Patrick must, then, at least be considered possible.

Before long Brigid was the head of a community of virgins; Ailerán mentions she was consecrated with eight other women, and presumably this number only increased as her fame spread. We see that by the time she constructed her abbey at Kildare, she was on familiar terms with the King of Leinster, who contributed a hundred loads of rods for the construction. It is a shame that neither Cogitosus nor Ailerán discuss the foundation of Kildare in greater detail. How many sisters lived there? Who were some of the early personalities that worked beside Brigid? What sort of rule did they organize themselves under? We can only speculate.

Likewise, Brigid's evangelical labors are glossed over with
the simple phrase that she had spent her life "founding
churches and church buildings in plenty." How we would like
to know more about which churches and buildings she erected!
Fr. John Colgan's 17th century hagiography *Acta Triadis
Thaumaturgae* suggests that many of these churches were in
Connacht in what is now the Diocese of Elpin.

Cogitosus records Brigid's death as February 1, but the
Leabhar Breac says she passed on the twenty-eighth. There
appears to be no explanation for this contradiction, but the date
of February 1 is of much weightier authority, as it was
established as Brigid's feast day within her living memory and
has remained such ever since. The *Vita I* of St. Ailerán describes
her death:

> After her victory saint Brigit departed this life
> amid choirs of patriarchs and prophets and
> apostles and martyrs and all the holy men and
> virgins and amid the ranks of angels and
> archangels to the eternal diadems of the
> heavenly kingdom, to the heavenly Jerusalem,
> to the kingdom without end where everlasting
> rewards are bestowed through Our Lord Jesus
> Christ together with the Father and Holy Spirit
> through endless ages. Amen.[8]

Brigid was buried beneath the high altar at the Cathedral of
Kildare, where she remained for three and a half centuries.

---

[8] S. Connolly, ed. and trans., *Vita Prima Sanctae Brigitae: Background
and Historical Value*, JRSAI, Vol. 119 (1989), p.49.

Around 878, as eastern Ireland began to come under control of the Vikings and churches were targeted for plunder, her remains were translated for safe keeping to Downpatrick in Ulster, where she was entombed beside Sts. Patrick and Columba, her saintly companions with whom she has been associated ever since.

She was succeeded as abbess by St. Darlugdach, her favorite pupil, whom she had once prevented from a sinful dalliance with a young man by putting hot coals in the young nun's shoes, burning Darlugdach's feet and preventing her from sneaking off.

Brigid's Miracles and Spirituality

Every *vita* of Brigid devotes ample space to her many miraculous works. Reading the miracles attributed to Brigid, one is struck with the rusticity of them. They reflect a deeply agricultural society: things such as the return of lost animals, replenishing depleted food stores, helping laborers move stones, and obtaining supernatural yields of milk and butter. Her most popular miracle—attested in Broccán, Cogitosus, Ailerán, and the *Bethu Brigte*—was when she milked a cow three times in a day and obtained three cows' worth of milk from that single animal.

Her reputation as an intercessor was well-established. The *Leabhar Breac* says:

> Many miracles and marvels in that wise the
> Lord wrought for Saint Brigit. Such is their
> number that no one could relate them unless

her own spirit, or an angel of God, should come
from heaven to relate them. For everything
which Brigit used to ask of the Lord used to
given to her at once.

It goes on to encourage her devotees to seek her intercession
for all manner of problems:

She is it that helpeth everyone who is in straits
and in danger. She it is that abateth the
pestilences. She it is that quelleth the wave-
voice and the wrath of the great sea. This is the
prophesied woman of Christ. She is the Queen
of the South. She is the Mary of the Gael.

The title "Mary of the Gael" is derived from a tale in *Vita I* and
has been a popular nickname for Brigid throughout the ages.
According to the story, a certain holy man at an episcopal
synod had a vision of the Blessed Virgin Mary coming across
the plain leading a company of virgins. Later, he goes out to the
Plain of Liffey and sees Brigid accompanied by her virgins
making her way to the synod. The man exclaimed "This is the
Mary that I beheld!" When Brigid arrives, she blesses everyone
in the name of the Virgin Mary. Ever after, the *Leabhar Breac*
tells us, she was known as "Mary of the Gael." The author of
the *Bethu Brigte*, writing centuries after *Vita I*, was apparently
uncomfortable with Brigid blessing the synod, as he reverses
the action: "The people of the assembly rose up before her and
went to converse with her. *They* blessed her."[9] The *Bethu Brigte*

---

[9] *Bethu Brigte*, Chapter 11. Translated by Donnchadh Ó hAodha
(University College: Cork, 2001)

also clarifies that Brigid's identification with Mary is merely symbolic: "Today a girl, for whom it has been prepared by God, will come to us *like* Mary."

The last stanza of "Broccán's Hymn" elevates Brigid above every other saint save the Blessed Virgin herself:

> I have not found like her save Mary...
> There are two nuns in the Kingdom—
> I implore their aid with all my effort—
> Mary and St. Brigid

Brigid's association with Mary can also be seen in her unique identification as the mystical mother of Jesus. In the second stanza of "Broccán's Hymn," Broccán calls Brigid, "mother of my high King, of the kingdom of heaven best." And in the conclusion of the *Leabhar Breac*, we see the following:

> This is the father of this holy virgin—the Heavenly Father. This is her son—Jesus Christ. This is her fosterer—the Holy Ghost.

Here the author of the *Leabhar Breac* draws upon classic Trinitarian and Marian theology to explain St. Brigid's relationship to God. But while it has been common in western Christendom for Christians to call God our Father and the Holy Spirit our helper or custodian, it is almost unheard of to call Jesus Christ "son," even among saintly women who imitate Mary's virtues exceptionally. This phraseology is not unique to the *Leabhar Breac*; we see the same language in "Broccán's Hymn":

she slept the sleep of a captive—
the saint, for the sake of her Son...
she was One-Mother of the Great King's Son

Historically, there has been a general Christian sensibility that the motherhood of Jesus is predicated of Mary uniquely—that, however perfectly a woman may model Mary spiritually, calling her Jesus's "mother" and He her "son" is a line never crossed. That Brigid's early biographers were at ease crossing this line is a peculiar eccentricity of Irish Catholicism, one that authors of later generations—like the author of *Bethu Brigte*—felt the need to carefully walk back from.

The spirituality of St. Brigid that emerges from the Brigittine corpus is of a woman consumed with desire for the works of mercy. *Leabhar Breac* says, "For this was her desire: to feed the poor, to repel every hardship, to be gentle to every misery." Sadly, the prevalent zeitgeist has chosen to reinterpret Brigid's activism as a kind of proto-feminism. Brigid's modesty would repel modern feminists. Again, the *Leabhar Breac*:

> Now there never hath been any one more bashful or more modest than that holy virgin. She never washed her hands, or her feet, or her head, amongst men. She never looked into a male person's face. She never spoke without blushing. She was abstinent, innocent, liberal, patient. She was joyous in God's commandments, steadfast, lowly, forgiving, and charitable. She was a consecrated vessel for keeping Christ's body. She was a temple of God. Her heart and her mind were a throne of rest

for the Holy Ghost. Towards God she was
simple; towards the wretched she was
compassionate; in miracles she was splendid.
Therefore, her type among created things is the
dove among birds, the vine among trees, the
sun above stars.

One of the worst perversions of St. Brigid's spirituality this
author has seen comes from those who enlist Brigid in the
cause of "reproductive rights." A 2018 article in the *Irish Post*
argues that St. Brigid "performed Ireland's first recorded
abortion."[10] That same year, religion professor Maeve Callan
authored a piece in the *Irish Times* entitled "Saints once did
abortions" and identified Brigid as one of Ireland's first
abortionists.[11] These arguments were made ahead of Ireland's
2018 referendum which lifted the country's ban on abortion by
an overwhelming margin. Why was Brigid held up as a beacon
of abortion rights?

The source of this assertion is a story in Cogitosus's *Vita II.*
He relates how Brigid "miraculously ended a pregnancy."
Cogitosus says:

A certain woman who had taken the vow of
chastity fell, through youthful desire of
pleasure, and her womb swelled with child.
Brigid, exercising the most potent strength of
her ineffable faith, blessed her, causing the

---

[10] Fiona Audley, "According to scripture St. Brigid performed the first
abortion in Ireland," *Irish Post*, February 5, 2018

[11] Maeve Callan, "Saints once did abortions—it was a lesser sin than oral
sex," *Irish Times*, April 19, 2018.

foetus to disappear, without coming to birth,
and without pain. She faithfully returned the
woman to health and to penance.

That this is nothing like an abortion should be immediately
apparent. An abortion is a medical procedure wherein there is
a deliberate destruction of the fetus resulting in its death.
St. Brigid here performs no procedure nor deliberately does
anything to bring about the child's death; rather, she blesses
the woman and commends the matter to God, in whose hands
are the power of life and death. Furthermore, this passage
cannot be taken to imply any sort of primitive support for
abortion from Brigid or the ancient Irish Church. St. Brigid's
actions here are meant to glorify God and preserve the honor
of a fallen woman, not affirm abortion on principle.

It is to be particularly lamented that St. Brigid has been
attached to causes that she would have repudiated during her
life. We shall explore this issue in much greater detail in the
appendix essay on the question of Brigit the goddess and the
saint's connection to paganism.

Brigid's Authority and Legacy

St. Brigid was of such renown that she had a vibrant cultus
while yet living. So widely was she respected that she was
able to choose which cleric would become bishop of her
newly established church at Kildare, selecting St. Conleth.
When she was on her deathbed, she was attended by
St. Ninnidh; this Ninnidh prepared her soul for death and
gave Brigid her last Holy Communion. After administering

the sacrament to the dying nun, St. Ninnidh kept his hand encased in a metal glove so it should never be defiled by touching anything else again. Ever after he was known as St. Ninnidh the Pure-Handed. These episodes should give some idea of the fame in which she was held; the *Leabhar Breac* does not exaggerate when it calls her "the Queen of the South."

The history of the Irish Church in the first millennium is one of fractious rivalry between various dioceses for preeminence. The most assertive claimant for supremacy was Armagh, the church founded by St. Patrick. Armagh's apologists were insistent that God had given jurisdiction of the entire island of Ireland to St. Patrick and his successors. Tírechán—the pupil of St. Ultan—would assert that every Irish community founded by a bishop should owe allegiance to Armagh. Tírechán was a contemporary of Cogitosus, and the latter may have written his *vita* of Brigid to counter the claims of Armagh by proclaiming the glories of St. Brigid, the renowned founder of Kildare. The miracles of Brigid and the bustling pilgrim center of Kildare described by Cogitosus demonstrated Kildare's ability to stand on its own without the interference of Armagh. Cogitosus, in fact, argues that Kildare, not Armagh, should have episcopal supremacy. In the prologue to *Vita II* he makes the stunning claim for Kildare that:

> It is the head of virtually all the Irish churches
> and occupies the first place, excelling all the

monasteries of the Irish. Its jurisdiction extends over the whole land of Ireland from sea to sea.[12]

The famous story of St. Brigid's episcopal "consecration" exemplifies the struggle of Kildare to assert an episcopal lineage independent of Patrick. The episode is well-attested in various *vitae*: St. Brigid goes to receive the veil at the hand of St. Mél, but Mél absent-mindedly reads the order of episcopal consecration instead. When his companion MacCaille protests that it is not proper to confer episcopal ordination upon a woman, St. Mél says, "No power have I in this matter, inasmuch as by God hath been given unto her this honour beyond every woman." There is no evidence that Brigid was ever actually regarded as a bishop in the strict sense (if she was, why did she need to recruit Conleth to serve as Kildare's bishop?), but that is beside the point—St. Mél's action is prophetic and portrayed as such. One of the prerogatives of bishops is to found churches. But Kildare, the most important church of Leinster—indeed, of all southern Ireland—was founded by St. Brigid, a nun. By what authority does Brigid found churches? Even though she does not have episcopal orders in the theological sense, the honor Mél confers on her through the prophetic witness of the Holy Ghost legitimizes Brigid's foundation of Kildare.

This is directly relevant to the rivalry with Armagh. Tírechán's apologias stated that every community founded by a bishop owed allegiance to Armagh. But Kildare was not

---

[12] Though Kildare did retain a supremacy over other Irish abbeys as the motherhouse of Irish monasticism, it never made good on its claims of episcopal jurisdiction over Ireland. The 1152 Synod of Kells, presided over by a papal legate, definitively affirmed the primacy of Armagh and made Kildare a suffragan of the Archbishop of Dublin.

founded by a bishop, and hence stood outside the episcopal lineage of Armagh. To draw a parallel with Eowyn in the *Lord of the Rings*, it was St. Brigid's "I am no man" moment.

Another effort to circumvent the claims of Armagh may have been in the selection of St. Conleth to serve as bishop of Kildare. St. Conleth was originally a hermit skilled in metalwork who had a reputation for piety and craftsmanship. Cogitosus describes Brigid's desire to take Conleth as bishop:

> Taking thought, she decided that she could not make her foundation without a high priest who could consecrate churches and confer orders on the clergy. She called on a famous hermit, distinguished in every way, a man through whom God made much goodness manifest, to leave his hermitage and his solitary life and to come and join her in that place so that he might rule the church with her in episcopal dignity, and so ensure that nothing of the priestly office would be lacking in her establishments.

Thus Conleth became Bishop of Kildare, to "rule the church with her in episcopal dignity." Thus Kildare ever after boasted a double line of abbesses and abbot-bishops, the abbesses governing the nuns and the abbot-bishops the monks.

But, if Brigid wished her foundation to stand outside the lineage of Armagh, then by whom was St. Conleth ordained to the episcopate? We are not told, but it is likely that he was ordained outside of Ireland, based on a tantalizing passage in Cogitosus. Commenting on an episode where St. Brigid gave away the bishop's vestments to a poor man, Cogitosus says:

> [Brigid] gave away to the poor the foreign and
> exotic robes of the illustrious bishop Conlaeth,
> vestments wore in the course of the liturgy of
> the Lord and the apostolic vigils.

Note that St. Conleth's episcopal vestments are described as
"foreign and exotic." Perhaps Conleth simply had exotic tastes
and purchased foreign vestments, but a likelier explanation is
that Conleth obtained episcopal consecration outside of Ireland.
We know that Armagh was making a determined effort to
subordinate all Irish dioceses to itself, and that Brigid wished
to resist this ecclesiastical aggrandizement. She may have sent
Conleth abroad for episcopal ordination so that his orders
would not stand in the lineage of Armagh. This could explain
why his vestments were foreign.

This might also shed light on the manner of Conleth's death.
The tale of Conleth's end is told in an obscure document called
the *Tract of Aengus the Culdee*, which relates how Conleth
wished to go to Rome. St. Brigid tried to dissuade him, and the
two had a falling out over the matter. Conleth departed against
her wishes, but before he had even left Ireland he was attacked
and killed by wolves on the road in 519.

Why did Conleth want to go to Rome? The records do not
say. But the learned Irish antiquarian, Rev. James H. Todd
(1805-1869), believed St. Conleth was making a *second* visit to
Rome at the time of his death.[13] Dr. Todd suggested Rome as
the place of Conleth's episcopal ordination when he assumed

---

[13] For more on this question, see John O' Hanlon, *Lives of the Irish Saints,
with Special Commemorations of Holy Persons*, Vol. V (Catholic
Publishing Society: New York, 1873) pp. 86-91

the see of Kildare in 490. Years later, perhaps to confer with the pope about matters of governance, perhaps to obtain more rare vestments to replace those Brigid gave away (being, as he was, a lover of fine craftsmanship), Conleth wished to return to Rome, did so against Brigid's admonition, and died en route. This is all conjecture, but it is certainly plausible: faced with the claims of Armagh to primacy, Brigid sent Conleth for ordination to the one place whose primacy Armagh could not possibly dispute—Rome.

Cogitosus relates that Brigid knew that "she could not make her foundation without a high priest who could consecrate churches and confer orders on the clergy." Thus, she recruited St. Conleth as her bishop, to "ensure that nothing of the priestly office would be lacking in her establishments." This passage should be sufficient to put to rest the oft-repeated assertion that Brigid herself acted as bishop over Kildare. If she fulfilled this role herself, why did she need St. Conleth? Further evidence that Brigid never fulfilled the role of bishop comes from the 9th century *Bethu Brigte* relates how a pagan named Seir asked Brigid for baptism after witnessing a miracle. Brigid assents to the man's baptism, but explains that she is not capable of administering the sacrament:

> "I do not mind provided that you be baptized,"
> said Brigit. "There is not a man in orders with
> me. Let someone go from us to Patrick, so that
> a bishop or priest may come to baptize this

man." Brón came and baptized the man with all
his household at sunrise.[14]

If she were an acting bishop, why did she need to fetch a priest
to administer baptism?

It is evident from the texts that Brigid never claimed nor
wielded actual sacerdotal jurisdiction of any kind. Yet such is
commonly asserted. The confusion probably arises from the
unique role historically played by the abbesses of Kildare.
Cogitosus states that Conleth was recruited "so that he might
rule the church with her in episcopal dignity." By virtue of
Brigid's renown, Kildare became a double-monastery, the
women presided over by an abbess and the men by an abbot,
who doubled as the Bishop of the Diocese of Kildare. While
double monasteries were common on the continent, Kildare
was the only known double-monastery in Ireland. Cogitosus
depicts Kildare as under the joint rule of Conleth and Brigid,
and while this is true, some distinctions must be observed.

First, that Kildare was both an abbey and a diocese.
St. Brigid and the abbesses of Kildare were the supreme
authorities over the abbey, while St. Conleth and the abbot-
bishops were supreme authorities over the diocese. When
Cogitosus says Conleth came "to rule the church with her in
episcopal dignity," he is not asserting that Brigid was
considered a bishop, nor that Conleth and Brigid shared the
episcopal office; rather, he is explaining that Brigid sought
Conleth as bishop to ennoble with episcopal dignity the church

---

14 *Bethu Brigte*, Chap. 41, trans. Donnchadh Ó hAodha (Dublin Institute
for Advanced Studies: Dublin, 1978), 32

that she had already founded. Cogitosus explains this beautifully when he says:

> [Conleth,] anointed principal of all the bishops, and Brigid, most blessed head of all the women, built their church in happy partnership, guided by virtue. Their episcopal and feminine see, like a fertile vine expanding everywhere in growing branches, spread throughout the whole island of Ireland.

Conleth provides the episcopal head, and Brigid the leadership over the women. It was a "happy partnership," a church endowed with both masculine and feminine properties—the masculine represented by the "episcopal," which complements the "feminine" aspect of the see. The episcopal pertains to its visible government, the feminine to its spiritual interior. Together, their combined gifts cause Kildare to flourish "like a fertile vine expanding everywhere."

Furthermore, we must understand the nature of diocesan administration in the early Irish church. In most of western Europe, abbots and bishops were distinct from one another. But in Ireland, a number of early bishops were simultaneously abbots. Their dual role meant they had administrative duties as well as abbatial responsibilities. As it was easy for the administrative needs of governance to intrude upon an abbot's spiritual duties, the administrative responsibilities were entrusted to another official called a *coarb*. Coarb means "heir," in the sense of successor to the saint who founded the church. The coarb was usually a lay person, although they could also be a tonsured religious. The coarbs were overseers of the temporalities of larger institutions; they procured supplies, collected rents, solicited donations, organized defense, and managed what we might today call the "business end" of church affairs. This freed up the bishop to attend to his sacramental, evangelical, and abbatial duties unhindered. This was the normative means of Irish diocesan management until the Norman invasion (1169).

The abbesses of Kildare fulfilled this role within the Diocese of Kildare. The histories speak of the abbesses of Kildare as the *"comarbae Brigte,"* literally, "the heirs (*coarbs*) of Brigid." As coarbs, the abbesses of Kildare would have wielded tremendous authority over the temporalities of church, but they were not above the bishop in the ecclesiastical hierarchy. There is no evidence that the abbesses of Kildare or any other woman exercised episcopal authority in medieval Ireland. Nevertheless, the misunderstanding seems to have already been present in the high Middle Ages. The *Leabhar Breac*, commenting on the episode with St. Mél, says, "Hence, it is that the men of Ireland give the honour of bishop to Brigit's successor." It is probable that the author of the *Leabhar Breac*—writing centuries after the office of coarb went extinct—misunderstood the nature of the coarb and the role played by Kildare's abbesses. This, combined with the episode of St. Mél's accidental "consecration," gave rise to the persistent legend that Brigid exercised episcopal authority.

That such legends were even told of Brigid reflects the intense esteem she was held in by the Irish. Her renown spread even outside Éire, as evidenced by the fascinating travels of St. Brigid's relics. As mentioned above, Brigid's relics were removed from Kildare in 878 and transferred to Downpatrick due to frequent Viking raids in Leinster. There she was reinterred beside St. Patrick and St. Columba. At this time, other relics were sent abroad as well (her teeth to Cologne, for example). Her body was moved again in 1185 when Downpatrick came under the control of John de Courcy, an Anglo-Norman knight who moved them to a more prominent place in Down Cathedral. During these translations, the head was divided up, the occipital lobe being given into the hands of some of Courcy's knightly vassals, while the bulk of the skull remained in the cathedral. The occipital lobe passed into the keeping of three knights (presumably brothers of a single family) who went to join the Aragonese Crusade in 1283. The knights, passing through Portugal, attracted the attention of King Dinis. The king, hearing they bore the precious skull of St. Brigid, entreated them to gift it to the crown and enshrine it in the newly constructed church at Lumiar. According to tradition, the knights refused to be parted from the relic, but agreed to King Dinis's request on condition that they be allowed to remain in Lumiar as caretakers of the holy skull.[15] And so they did. To this day in the church of Lumiar, there can be seen three tombs, which bear this inscription:

> Here in these three tombs lie the three Irish knights who brought the head of St. Brigid, Virgin, a native of Ireland, whose relic is preserved in this chapel. In memory of which,

---

[15] It should be noted there are multiple versions of this story in circulation, some which say the knights were killed in battle, others that they died of plague.

the officials of the Altar of the same Saint caused this to be done in January AD 1283.

Opposite the tomb inscription, the occipital lobe of Brigid is still preserved inside a golden reliquary in a wall niche behind an iron grille.

The main repository of Brigid's relics remained in Down Cathedral until the time of Henry VIII. In 1538, during the tumults accompanying Lord Grey's tenure as Lord Deputy of Ireland, the remains were desecrated by the English. The head of Brigid, however, was preserved by some faithful clergy, who spirited it away to a Franciscan monastery in Neustadt, Austria. There it became a treasured relic of the Holy Roman Emperors. In 1587, Emperor Rudolf II bestowed the skull as gift to the Jesuit church of Igreja de São Roque in Lisbon, Portugal then being under the rule of Rudolf's maternal uncle, Philip II. The skull remains in an altar reliquary within the church of São Roque to this day, minus a fragment that was returned to Ireland by the Archbishop of Lisbon in 1929.[16]

Some Notes on the Text

I am indebted to the work of the Irish scholar Dr. Whitley Stokes (1830-1909), without whose patient labors so much knowledge of the ancient Irish church would remain untranslated. "Broccán's Hymn" and "Ultan's Hymn" first appeared in English in the 1892 *Goidelica: Old and Early Middle-Irish Glosses*, an encyclopedic resource edited by Dr. Stokes. He

---

[16] We should also mention that a section of St. Brigid's cloak remains preserved at Bruges in Belgium.

also gave us the translation of the *Leabhar Breac* in his earlier work *Three Middle Irish Homilies* (1877). I am indebted to George Petrie (1790-1866), whose 1833 translations of Cogitosus for the Royal Irish Academy were extremely helpful; also, the records of the 1867 *Irish Ecclesiastical Record* (published by Browne and Nolan) and, especially, the translations of Cogitosus in the *Saintly Triad* of Robert Rochford (c. 1625), and of Father John Colgan (d. 1658).

I would also like to give especial thanks to Marcella, an Irish laywoman and devotee of St. Brigid who has been blogging about the saint of Kildare for the past ten years. Her blog, *Trias Thaumaturga*, contains a wealth of resources on St. Brigid, including excerpts of a great many scholarly works modern and antique. If it was not for her, I would not have discovered Whitley Stokes's translations of Ultan and Broccán.

The reader will notice that the name of our saint is spelled variously throughout the text, appearing sometimes as Brigit, other times as Brigid, and occasionally as Brigte or Bridgit. These variations can all be found in the original source material, and I have chosen to preserve them in their respective sections. For the original content of the book, I have chosen to use the spelling Brigid, as this was that preferred by Cogitosus.

On a personal note, publishing this modest collection of literature on the life of St. Brigid has been a passion of mine for many years now. At the time of writing, it has probably been over a decade since I first began collecting resources on the great saint of Kildare; it was only the vagaries of circumstance that prevented me for so long from realizing this dream. But now that it is realized, I pray, to God and

St. Brigid, that her splendor may again be radiant across many lands, and that, in a special way, she would intercede for the soul of her beloved homeland. May the Spirit empower me to write worthily of this most excellent woman.

Phillip Campbell
August 10, 2022
Feast of St. Lawrence, Deacon and Martyr

Homily From
The *Leabhar Breac*

hese are the folk that follow the unpolluted Lamb, whatsoever way He may wend. John, Son of Zebedee, Jesus' bosom-fosterling, heir of the Virgin, he it is that wrote these words, and that left them in the Church Christian in memory of the reward and guerdon which God hath given to the third grade of the Church, namely, to the Virgins, that is, the following of the unpolluted Lamb. Now this is the parallel part of the declaration by John, as far as where he previously said in his Gospel. There cometh not to any one on earth to make unto the Lord meet praise or fitting quire-song, save only of a surety one of the all-fullness of either Church, who hath been brought up in chastity and in virginity, and hath been redeemed with the price of Christ's blood. For those are the virgins assuredly. So on the track of these words John saith, it profiteth not any one to have the flesh a virgin if he be corrupt in mind. For this is in the Gospel, that these are the virgins that have not oil in their vessels, namely, the virgins that do not keep (to themselves) the approbation of the Lord, but (make) boasting before everyone.

Now Patriarchs fulfilled the testament of virginity in prefiguration of Christ. And apostles and disciples of Jesus Christ son of the living God fulfilled it also, the martyrs and anchorites of the Lord, the saints and holy virgins of the world besides, even as the holy, venerable virgin fulfilled it, she that hath a festival and commemoration on the occasion of this season and this time, to wit, the holy virgin of God, Brigit, for then it is that the Christians celebrate the feast and festal day of this holy Brigit, to wit, the Kalends of February as to the day of the solar month.

Here then is related in the churches of the Christians somewhat of her miracles and marvels, and of her birth according to flesh—

Brigit was the daughter of Dubthach, son of Demre (or Dreimne), son of Bresal, son of Den, son of Conla, son of Artair, son of Art Corb, son of Cairpe the Champion, son of Cormac, son of Oengus the Dumb, son of Eochaid Find Fuathnart, son of Fedlimid the Lawgiver.

Now, that Dubthach son of Demre bought a bondmaid, named Broicsech, daughter of Dallbrónach of Dál Conchobair in the south of Bregia. Dubthach united himself in wedlock to her, and she became pregnant by him. Thereafter Dubthach's consort grew jealous of the bondmaid (Brechtnat Blaithbec was the name of Dubthach's wife) and the queen said, "Unless thou sellest this bondmaid in far-off lands, I will demand my dowry of thee, and I will go from thee."

But Dubthach did not at all desire to sell the bondmaid. So Dubthach went, and his bondmaid along with him, in a chariot, past the house of a certain wizard. When the wizard heard the noise of the chariot, this he said: "See, O gillie [servant], who is in the chariot, for this is the noise of a chariot under a king."

Said the gille, "Dubthach is therein." Then the wizard went to
meet the chariot, and he asked whose was the woman who was
biding in the chariot. Said Dubthach, "That is a bondmaid of
mine," quoth he. Maithgen was the wizard's name, and from
him Ross Maithgen is named. The wizard asked by whom the
bondmaid was pregnant. "By Dubthach," said the bondmaid.
Said the wizard, "Marvelous will be the offspring, the like of
her will not be in all the lands."

Said Dubthach, "My consort did not allow me not to sell
this bondmaid."

Said the wizard through his gift of prophecy, "Thy wife's
seed shall serve this bondmaid's seed, for the bondmaid will
bring forth a daughter, noble, revered, before the men of the
earth. As sun shineth among stars, so will shine the maiden's
deeds and merits."

Dubthach and the bondmaid rejoiced thereat, and
Dubthach said, "Since I have already sons, I should like to have
a daughter." Then Dubthach returned to his house and his
bondmaid with him. The wife however was still jealous of the
bondmaid.

Great was the honour in which God held this girl. For two
bishops of the Britons came to her from Alba to prophesy of
her and to sanctify her, to wit, Bishop Mél and Melchu. So
Dubthach gave them a welcome and the bondmaid served them
and tended them. Now Dubthach's consort was mournful
thereat, and Bishop Mél asked her the cause of her sadness.

Then responded the wife, "Because Dubthach doth
distinguisheth his bondmaid from me." Said Bishop Mél, "Thus
shall it be as thou sayest, for thy seed shall serve the seed of the
bondmaid, but with her seed shall be profitable unto thy seed."
She was angry with him. So the bishop asked her, "How many

sons hast thou?" Said the wife, "Six sons." Said Bishop Mél, "Thou shalt bear the seventh son, and he will be the worst of them, and the other sons will be bad unless the bondmaid's seed ennobles them, and thou thyself shalt be accursed because of the wrong which thou doest to the bondmaid."

After those words there came to Dubthach's house, out of the border of Ui-Maiccuais, another wizard who had been gathering treasures. Now when the wizard knew that the bondmaid was the cause of the anger of Dubthach's wife, he said, "Wilt thou sell the bondmaid?" "I will sell," saith Dubthach. Quoth the bishops, "Sell the bondmaid, but sell not the child that is in her womb." Thus did Dubthach.

The wizard went forth and the bondmaid with him. The wizard with his bondmaid arrived at his house.

A certain poet came out of the province of Conaille to the house of the wizard aforesaid in order to buy a slave or a bondmaid. The wizard sold him the bondmaid, but sold him not the offspring. Then it came to pass that the wizard made a great feast, and bade the king of Conaille to the feast, and it was then the time for the king's wife to bear a child. There was a prophet along with the king, and a friend of the king's asked him what hour would be lucky for the queen to bring forth the royal offspring. Said the prophet, "The child that shall be brought forth to-morrow at sunrise shall overtop every birth in Ireland." Now the queen's travail came on before that hour, and she brought forth a dead son. Then the poet asked the prophet what hour would be lucky for the bondmaid to bring forth? Said the poet, "The child that shall be brought forth to-morrow at sunrise, and neither within the house nor without, shall surpass every child in Ireland."

Now on the morrow, at sunrise, when the bondmaid was going with a vessel full of milk in her hand, and when she put one foot over the threshold of the house inside and the other foot outside, then did she bring forth the girl, to wit, Brigit.

The maidservants washed the girl with the milk that was in her mother's hand. Now that was in accord with the merits of Saint Brigit, to wit, with the brightness and sheen of her chastity. On a Wednesday and in the eighth moon was Brigit born in Fothart Murthemni. Still, to the south-east of the church is the flagstone whereon Brigit was born, and the girl was taken straightway after her birth to the queen's dead son, and when Brigit's breath came to him he swiftly arose out of death.

Then the wizard and the bondmaid with her daughter went into the province of Connaught (her mother was of Connaught, her father out of Munster, her abode with the Connaughtmen).

On a certain day the bondmaid went to her island and covered up her daughter in her house. Certain neighbors saw the house wherein was the girl all ablaze, so that a flame of fire was made of it from earth to heaven. But when they went to rescue the house, the fire appeared not, and this they said, that the girl was full of the Holy Spirit.

One day the wizard went with his bondmaid to visit the cattle. The cow-dung that lay before the girl was seen ablaze. But when the wizard and the bondmaid stretched down their hands to it, the fire appeared not.

Once upon a time when the wizard was sleeping, he saw three clerics in white garments, to wit, three angels of heaven, and they poured oil on St. Brigit's head, and they, completed the order of baptism. And the third cleric said to the wizard

"This shall be the name of this holy maiden: *Sancta Brigita.*"
The wizard arose and told what he had beheld.

Now this holy virgin, namely, Brigit, was nourished with
food and like to her compeers (?) besides, and she rejected the
guidance of the wizard and used to give it (the food) away. The
wizard meditated on the girl, and it seemed to him that it was
because of the impurity and the corruption of his food. Then he
enjoined a white red-eared cow to give milk to Brigit, and he
enjoined a faithful woman to milk the cow. The virgin took her
fill of that.

That holy virgin was reared till she was a handmaiden, and
everything to which her hand was set used to increase and
reverence God. Every store of food which she saw and served
used to grow. She bettered the sheep, she tended the blind, and
she fed the poor.

Thereafter Brigit was minded to depart and watch over her
fatherland. And the wizard sent messengers to Dubthach, that
he might come for his daughter. The messengers declared unto
Dubthach the maiden's miracles and many wonders. Then
Dubthach came, and the wizard bade him welcome, and gave
him his daughter free.

Then they went to their country, Dubthach and his
daughter Brigit, in the province of Offaly and there did Brigit
work a wondrous miracle, to wit, her fostermother was in
weakness of disease, and the fostermother sent the holy
Brigit and another maiden with her to the house of a certain
man named Boethchu, to ask him for a draught of ale. He
refused Brigit. Then Brigit filled a vessel out of a certain well,
and blessed it, and the water was turned into the taste of ale,
and she gave it to her fostermother, who straightway became

whole thereby. Now when they went to drink the banquet not a drop thereof was found.

This (was another) of Brigit's miracles: while she was herding Dubthach's swine, there came two robbers and carried off two boars of the flock. They fared over the plain, and Dubthach met them and bound on them the *erc* (mulct) of his swine. Said Dubthach to Brigit, "Is the herding of the swine good, my girl?" saith he. Said Brigit to Dubthach, "Count thou the swine." Dubthach counted the swine, and not one of them was wanting.

Guests, then, came to Dubthach. Dubthach sundered a gammon of bacon into five pieces, and left them with Brigit to be boiled. And a miserable, greedy hound came into the house to Brigit. Brigit out of pity gave him the fifth piece. When the hound had eaten that piece Brigit gave another piece to him. Then Dubthach came and said to Brigit: "Hast thou boiled the bacon, and do all the portions remain?" "Count them," saith Brigit. Dubthach counted them, and none of them was wanting.

The guests declared unto Dubthach what Brigit had done. "Abundant," saith Dubthach, "are the miracles of that maiden." Now the guests ate not the food, for they were unworthy (thereof), but it was dealt out to the poor and to the needy of the Lord.

Once upon a time a certain faithful woman asked Dubthach that Brigit might go with her into the plain of the Liffey, for a congregation of the synod of Leinster was held there. And it was revealed in a vision to a certain holy man who was in the assembly, that Mary the Virgin was coming thereto, and it was told him that she would not be accompanied by a man in the assembly. On the morrow came the woman to the assembly, and Brigit along with her. And he that had seen the vision said,

"This is the Mary that I beheld" saith he to Brigit. The holy Brigit blessed all the hosts under the name and honor of Mary. Wherefore Brigit was called "the Mary of the Gael" thenceforward.

On a time it came into Brigit's mind, through the grace of the Holy Ghost, to go and see her mother who was in bondage. So she asked her father's leave, and he gave it not. Nevertheless, she went without permission from Dubthach. Glad was her mother when she arrived. Toil-worn and sickly was the mother and she (Brigit) for her mother, and took to bettering the dairy. The first churning that Brigit had she divided the fruit thereof into twelve shares in honor of the twelve apostles of the Creator, and she set the thirteenth portion so that it was greater than every other portion in honor of Jesus Christ, and she gave them all then to the poor of the Lord. Now the wizard's herdsman marveled at the ordering that Brigit gave the butter. Then said Brigit: "Christ with his twelve apostles preached to the men of the world. In His name it is that I feed the poor, for Christ is in the person of every faithful poor man."

The charioteer (that is the herdsman) went to the wizard's house, and the wizard and his wife asked him "Hath the virgin well cared for the dairy?" And the charioteer (i.e., the herdsman) said "I am thankful anyhow, and the calves are fat" for he dared not carp at Brigit in her absence. The charioteer took with him a firkin, [a cask for butter] eight fists in height. Said the charioteer to Brigit: "The wizard will come with his wife to fill this firkin with the butter of the dairy." "They are welcome," saith Brigit. The wizard and his consort came to the dairy and beheld the calves fat. And Brigit made them welcome and brought them food. Then said the wizard's wife to Brigit: "We have come to know whether that which hath been entrusted to thee hath profited. Of butter what hast thou?" She had none in readiness, except the making of one churning and a half making, and she first brought the half. The wizard s wife mocked thereat and said: "This quantity of butter," says she, "is good to fill the big firkin that I have." "Fill your firkin," saith Brigit, "and God will put butter into it."

So she kept going still into her kitchen and carrying out of it a half making at every journey, for God did not wish to deprive her of honor, so in that wise the firkin was filled. And this is what she repeated on going into her kitchen:

> O God, O my Prince
> Who canst do all these things,
> Bless, O God, a cry unforbidden,
> With thy right hand this kitchen!
> May Mary's Son, my Friend, come
> To bless my kitchen!
> The Prince of the world to the border,
> May we have abundance with Him!

After this, the wizard and his consort venerated the Lord because of the miracle which they beheld; wherefore then said the wizard to Brigit: "The butter and the kine that thou hast milked, I offer them to thee. Thou shalt not abide in bondage to me, but serve thou the Lord." Brigit answered him and said: "Take thou the kine and give me my mother's freedom." Said the wizard: "Not only shall thy mother be freed, but the kine shall be given to thee, and whatsoever thou shalt say, that will I do." Then Brigit dealt out the kine unto the poor and the needy of God. The wizard was baptized and was faithful and accompanied Brigit from that time forth.

Then came Brigit, and her mother with her, to her father's house. Thereafter Dubthach and his consort were minded to sell the holy Brigit into bondage; for Dubthach liked not his cattle and his wealth to be dealt out to the poor, and that is what Brigit used to do. So Dubthach fared in his chariot, and Brigit along with him. Said Dubthach to Brigit: "Not for honor or reverence to thee art thou carried in a chariot, but to take thee to sell thee, and to grind the handmill for Dunlang MacEnda, King of Leinster." When they came to the King s fortress, Dubthach went into the King and Brigit remained in her chariot at the fortress door. Dubthach had left his sword in the chariot near Brigit. A leper came to Brigit to ask alms. She gave him Dubthach's sword. Said Dubthach to the King: "Wilt thou buy a bondmaid, namely, my daughter?" says he. Said Dunlang to Dubthach: "What causes thou to sellest thou thine own daughter?" Replied Dubthach: "She stayeth not from selling my wealth and giving it to the poor." Said the King: "Let the maiden come into the fortress." Dubthach went for Brigit and was enraged against her, because she had given his sword to the poor man. When Brigit came into the King's presence, the King said to her: "Since it is thy father's wealth that thou takest, much more, if I buy thee, wilt thou take my wealth and my cattle and give them to the poor?" Said Brigit: "The Son of the Virgin knoweth if I had thy might with all Leinster, and with all thy wealth I would give them to the Lord of the Elements." Said the King to Dubthach: "Thou art not fit on either hand to bargain about this maiden, for her merit is higher before God than before men." And the King gave Dubthach for her an ivory-hilled sword, and thus the holy virgin Brigit was freed from captivity.

Shortly after that came a certain nobleman unto Dubthach to ask for his daughter in marriage. Dubthach and his sons were willing, but Brigit refused. Said a brother of her brethren named Beccan unto her: "Idle is the fair eye that is in thy head not to be on a pillow near a husband."

"The Son of the Virgin knows," says Brigit, "it is not lively for us if it brings harm upon us." Then Brigit put her finger under her eye and drew it out of her head till it was on her cheek; and she said: "Lo, here for thee is thy delightful eye, O Beccan!" Then his eye burst forthwith. When Dubthach and her brethren beheld that, they promised that she should never be told to go unto a husband. Then she put her palm to her eye and it was quite whole at once. But Beecan's eye was not whole till his death.

Said Dubthach to Brigit: "O daughter," says he, "put a veil on thy head. If thou hast dedicated thy virginity to God, I will not snatch it from Him." Says Brigit, "Deo gratias,."

Brigit, and certain virgins with her, went to Bishop Mél, in Telcha Mide, to take the veil. Glad was he thereat. For humbleness Brigit staid, so that she might be the last to whom the veil should be given. A fiery pillar arose from her head to the ridgepole of the church. Bishop Mél asked: "What virgin is there?" Answered MacCaille: "That is Brigit," saith he. "Come thou, O holy Brigit," saith Bishop Mél, "that the veil may be sained on thy head before other virgins."

It came to pass then, through the grace of the Holy Ghost, that the form of ordaining a bishop was read over Brigit. MacCaille said that "The order of a bishop should not be conferred on a woman." Said Bishop Mél: "No power have I in this matter, inasmuch as by God hath been given unto her this honour beyond every woman." Hence, it is that the men of Ireland give the honour of bishop to Brigit's successor.

In the eighth day of the lunar month was she born. On the eighteenth did she take the veil on her head. On the twenty-eighth did she go to heaven. Together with eight virgins was Brigit consecrated. According to the number of the eight beatitudes of the gospel did she fulfill her course. Still remaineth the altar's leg that lay in Brigit's hand though the three other legs were burnt.

This was one of Brigit's miracles. When the solemnity of Easter drew nigh, Brigit set up, shortly before Maunday-Thursday, in a certain place near unto Bishop Mél. Brigit desired, through her charity, to brew ale for the many churches that were around her, and it was not usual to brew ale at that time. Brigit possessed only one measure of malt, and Brigit's family had no vessels save two troughs. They made a tub of one of the two vessels, and they filled the other vessel with ale, and the virgins kept taking the ale from Brigit to the churches, and still the vessel before Brigit remained full. And thus, the produce of one measure of malt, through Brigit's blessing, supplied seven churches of Fir Telach for Maundy Thursday and for the eight days of Easter.

When the solemnity of Easter was fulfilled, Brigit asked her maidens whether they had the leavings of the Easter ale. Replied the virgins: "God will give food," say they. Then two maidens came in with a tub full of water. "The Virgin's Son knoweth," says Brigit, "that there is good ale there." She thought that it was ale. Quicker than speech, as she said that, the water was turned into choice ale forthwith.

Brigit went to a certain church in the land of Teffia to celebrate Easter, when on Maundy Thursday Brigit took to washing the feet of the old men and the feeble folk who were in the church. Four of the sick people there, among whom were a consumptive man, a madman, a blind man, and a leper. Brigit washed the feet of the four, and they were straightway healed from every disease that was on them.

Once Brigit was in a house as a guest, and all went out save a stripling of fourteen years. He had never spoken, nor moved foot or hand, and Brigit knew not that he was thus. So then came guests into the house to Brigit. Said Brigit to the stripling: "Attend on the guests." "I will do so," saith the stripling. He got up at once and did the service to the guests, and he was quite whole thenceforward.

Then there came to pass a meeting of the men of Ireland in Tailtin, in the place where Patrick abode, with a synod of Ireland's clerics around him. Now Brigit and Bishop Mél went to the meeting, and a certain woman also went thither with a babe on her arm, and she said that the babe was by Bishop Brón. The bishop, however, denied that. Brigit asked the woman by whom had she conceived the child, and told her not to utter a lie. And the woman answered: "It is by Bishop Brón." Then a swelling straightway filled her tongue, so that she was unable to speak. Brigit made the sign of the cross over the infant's mouth and asked it: "Who is thy father?" The infant answered and said "A wretched man who is in the outskirts of the assembly, that is my father," saith he. So in that wise Bishop Brón was saved through the grace of Brigit.

Brigit went to converse with St. Patrick in Mag Lemne while he was preaching the gospel. And Brigit fell asleep at the preaching. Said Patrick: "Wherefore hast thou slept?" Brigit bent her knees thrice and said: "I saw a vision," quoth she. Said Patrick: "Tell us the vision." "I saw," quoth she, "four ploughs in the south-east, and they ploughed the whole island, and before the sowing was finished the harvest grew up, and clear well-springs and shining streams came out of the furrows, and white garments were round the sowers and ploughmen. I beheld four other ploughs in the north, and they ploughed the island athwart, and before the harvest came again, the oats which they had sown grew up at once and ripened, and black streams came out of the furrows and black garments were on the sowers and on the ploughmen. And I was sorrowful thereat," quoth Brigit.

Said Patrick: "Be not in sadness, for good is that which thou beheld. The first four ploughs which thou beheld, those are I and thou. We sow the four books of the gospel with seed of faith and confession. The harvest which appeared to thee, that is the perfect faith of those men-folk. The four other ploughs, those are the false teachers and the liars, and they will overturn the teachings that we sow, and those we shall not uplift. But we, I and thou, shall then be in the presence of the Creator."

Then Brigit went to Dunlaing to ask him to forfeit to her father the sword which he had given to him while he was in the doorway of the fortress. Then a slave of the slaves of the King came to speak with Brigit and said to her: "If thou wouldst save me from servitude wherein I am, I would become a Christian and I would serve thee." Brigit said: "I will ask that of the King." So Brigit went into the fortress and asked her two boons of the King—the forfeiture of the sword to Dubthach, and his freedom for the slave. Said Brigit to the King: "If thou desirest excellent children and a kingdom for thy sons and Heaven for thyself, give me the two boons that I ask." Said the King to Brigit: "The kingdom of Heaven, as I see it not, and as no one knows what thing it is, I seek not, and a kingdom for my sons I seek not, for I should not myself be extant, and let each...[the manuscript here is unclear]...work in his time. But give me length of life in my kingdom and victory always over the Uí Néill, for there is often warfare between us. And give me victory in the first battle, so that I may be trustful in the other fights." And this was fulfilled in the battle of Lochar, which he fought against the Uí Néill.

Once upon a time the King of Leinster came unto Brigit to listen to preaching and celebration at Easter day. After the ending of the form of celebration, the King fared forth on his way and Brigit went to refection. Lommán, Brigit's leper, said he would eat nothing until the armor of the King of Leinster were given to him—both spears and sword and shield that he might move to and fro thereunder. A messenger went from Brigit after the King. From mid-day to evening was the King astray and he attained not even a thousand paces, so the armor was given by him, and bestowed on the leper.

Once upon a time Bishop Ercc and Brigit were in the land of Leinster. She said to Bishop Ercc: "There is at present a battle between thy tribe and its neighbors." Said a student of Bishop Ercc's family: "We think not," saith he, "that that is true." Brigit made the sign of the cross upon the student's eyes. Said the student: "I see my brothers a-slaughtering now." Then the student repented greatly.

Once upon a time a certain leper came to Brigit to ask for a cow. Said Brigit to him: "Which wouldst thou prefer, to carry off a cow or to be healed of the leprosy?" The leper said, that he would rather be healed of his leprosy than have the kingdom of all the world, for "every sound man is a king," saith he. Then Brigit made prayer to God and the leper was healed and served Brigit afterwards.

Now, when Brigit's fame in miracles and marvels had travelled throughout all Ireland, there came unto Brigit for their healing two blind men from Britain, and a little leper boy with them, and they put trust in Bishop Mél to get them healed. Said Brigit: "Let them stay outside just now till mass is over." Said the Britons (for those people are hasty), "You healed folk of thy own race yesterday, though you heal not us today." Brigit made prayer and the three were healed at once.

Brigit went afterwards with her virgins to Ardachad of Bishop Mél. The king of Teffia was at a feast near them. There was a vessel covered with many gems in the king's hand. And a certain careless man took it out of his hand, and it fell and broke into pieces. That man was seized by the king. Bishop Mél went to ask for him, but nothing could be got from the king save his death. However, Bishop Mél asked that the broken vessel might be given to him by the king, and then he had it and took it with him to the house wherein was Brigit. And Brigit made prayer to the Lord, and the vessel was restored in a form that was better than before, and then it was taken to the king, and the captive was loosed. And Bishop Mél said: "Not for me has God wrought this miracle, but for Brigit."

Once upon a time Brigit went to watch over a certain virgin, namely, the other Brigit, the daughter of Congaile, who used to work many miracles. And when Brigit and her virgins were at dinner, Brigit paused in the middle of the meal, and she said to a certain virgin: "Make thou Christ's cross over thy face and over thine eyes that you may see what I see." So then the virgin beheld Satan beside the table with his head down and his feet up, his smoke and his flame out of his gullet and out of his nostrils. Said Brigit to the demon that he should answer her:

"I cannot, O nun, be without conversing with thee, for truly thou keepest all of God's commandments! Moreover, thou art compassionate to God's poor and to His family."

"Tell us," said Brigit, "why are you hurtful in thy deeds to the human race?"

Said the demon: "That the race may not attain unto Paradise."

Said Brigit to the demon: "Wherefore hast thou come to us among our nuns?"

"A certain pious virgin is here," saith the demon, "and in her company am I."

Said Brigit to the virgin: "Put Christ's cross over thine eyes." And the virgin beheld at once the hideous monster there, and great fear seized the virgin when she beheld the demon.

"Wherefore shunnest thou," said Brigit, "the fosterling whom thou hast been cherishing for long seasons?" Then the virgin repented, and she was healed of the devil of gluttony and lust that had dwelt in her company.

Once upon a time Brigit went over to Teffia, and there were great hosts along with her. There were two lepers behind them, who quarreled on the road. The hand of him that first raised his hand withered, and then the hand of the other leper withered. Thereafter they repented and Brigit cured them of their leprosy.

Once upon a time Brigit with her virgins, was at Armagh, and two went by her bearing a tub of water. They came to Brigit to be blessed, and the tub fell behind them and went back over back from the door of the Rath as far as Loch Lapan. And it broke not, and not a drop fell thereout. It was well known to everyone that Brigit's blessing had caused this, and St. Patrick said: "Deal out the water throughout Armagh and Airthir."

So it was dealt, and it cured every disease and every ailment that was in the land.

Brigit went into the province of Fir Ross to loosen a captive who was *in manu* [i.e., a slave] with the King of Ross. Said Brigit: "Wilt thou set that captive free for me?" The King replied: "Though thou shouldst give me the realm of the men of Breg, I would not give him to thee. But go not with a refusal," saith the King. "For one night thou shalt have the right to guard his life for him." Then Brigit appeared at the close of day to the captive and said to him: "When the chain shall be opened for thee repeat this hymn, *Nunc populus*, and turn to thy right hand and flee." Thus it was done, and the captive fled at the word of Brigit.

Brigit one day came over Sliab Breg. There was a madman on the mountain who used to harry the companies who passed through the place. Great fear seized the virgins who were near Brigit, when they saw the madman. Said Brigit to the demoniac: "Since thou hast gone there, preach the word of God to us." "I cannot," he said, "be ungentle to thee, for thou are merciful to the Lord's family, to wit, to the poor and to the wretched." So then said the madman: "Reverence the Lord, O nun, and everyone will reverence thee, love the Lord, and everyone will love thee, fear the Lord and everyone will fear thee!" Then the madman went from them and did no hurt to them.

Brigit was one journeying in Mag Laigen, and she saw running past her a student, namely Ninnid the scholar.

"What art thou doing, O Sage!" saith Brigit, "and whither art thou wending so quickly?"

"To heaven," saith the scholar.

"The son of the Virgin knoweth," said Brigit, "that I would fain fare with thee!"

Said the scholar: "O nun, hinder me not from my road, or, if thou hinderest, beseech the Lord with me that the journey to heaven may be happy, and I will beseech God with thee that it may be easy for thee and that thou mayst bring many thousands with thee to heaven."

Brigit repeated a Paternoster with him, and he was pious thenceforward; and Brigit said that neither gallows nor punishment would be for him, and he it is that afterwards administered communion and sacrifice to Brigit.

Brigit went to Bishop Ibair that he might mark out her city for her. So they came thereafter to the place where Kildare is today. That was the season and the time that Ailill son of Dunlaing, with a hundred horse-loads of peeled rods, chanced to be going through the ground of Kildare.[17] Two girls came from Brigit to ask for some of the rods, and they got a refusal. Forthwith all the horses were struck down under their loads against the ground. Stakes and wattles were taken from them, and they arose not until Ailill son of Dunlaing had offered unto Brigit those one hundred horse-loads; and thereout was built Saint Brigit's house in Kildare.

> Then said Brigit—
> ... my house
> ...
> Let the kingship of Leinster forever be
> From Ailill son of Dunlaing.[18]

---

[17] Ailill Mac Dunlaing, King of Leinster (r. 495-527)
[18] Lacuna in the mansucript

On a time came two lepers unto Brigit to ask for alms. Nought else was in the kitchen save a single cow. So Brigit gave the single cow to the lepers. One of the two lepers gave thanks unto God for the cow. But the other leper was unthankful, for he was haughty.

"I alone," saith he, "have been sat at nought with a cow! Till today," saith he, "O ye nuns, I have never been counted among Culdees and amongst the poor and feeble, and I should not be treated like them with a single cow."[19]

Said Brigit to the lowly leper: "Stay thou here to see whether God will put anything into the kitchen, and let that haughty leper fare forth with his cow." Then came a certain heathen having a cow for Brigit. So Brigit gave that cow to the lowly leper. And when the haughty leper went on his way he was unable to drive his cow alone, so came back again to Brigit and to his comrade and was reviling and blaming Brigit. "Not for God's sake," saith he, "did you bestow this offering, but for mischief and oppressiveness thou gavest to me."

Thereafter the two lepers come to the Barrow. The river rose up against them. Through Brigit's blessing the lowly leper escaped with his cow. But the haughty leper fell in the stream, and his cow after him, and was drowned.

Once upon a time the Queen of Cremthan, son of Ennae Cennselach, that is, the queen of Leinster, came and brought a chain of silver to Brigit as an offering. The semblance of a human shape was at one of its ends, and an apple of silver on the other end. Brigit gave it to her virgins, they stored it up

---

[19] The Culdees (*Céilí Dé*, "Spouses of God") were an Irish ascetical movement organized in loose associations of hermits. As they did not arise until the 8th century, their mention here is anachronistic.

without her knowledge, for greatly used Brigit to take her wealth and give it to the poor. Nevertheless, a leper came to Brigit, and without her virgins' knowledge, she went to the chain and gave it to him. When the virgins knew this, they said, with much angry bitterness and wrath, "Little good have we from thy compassion to everyone," say they, "and we ourselves in need of food and raiment."

"Ye are sinning," saith Brigit: "Go ye into the church; the place wherein I make prayer, there will ye find your chain." They went at Brigit's word. But, though it had been given to the poor man, the virgins found their chain therein.

Once upon a time Brigit beheld a man with salt on his back. "What is that on thy back?" saith Brigit: "Stones," saith the man. "They shall be stones then," saith Brigit, and of the salt stones were made. The same man returned to Brigit. "What is that on thy back?" saith Brigit. "Salt," saith the man. "It shall be salt then," saith Brigit. Salt was made again thereof through Brigit's word.

On a time came two lepers unto Brigit to be healed. Said Brigit to one of the lepers: "Wash thou the other." Thus was it done, and he was quite sound forthwith. Said Brigit to the sound leper: "Bathe and wash thy comrade even as he did service unto thee." "Besides the time we have [already] come together," said he, "we will never come together, for it is not fair for thee, O nun, to expect me, a sound man with fresh limbs and fresh clean raiment, to wash that loathsome leper there, with his livid limbs falling out of him." However, Brigit herself washed the poor, lowly leper. The haughty leper who had been washed first, then spake, "Meseems," saith he, "that sparks of fire are breaking through my skin." Swifter than speech he was straightway smitten with leprosy from the crown of his head to his soles, because of his disobedience to Brigit.

Another time as Brigit was going to receive the sacrament from the bishop there was shewn to her a he-goat's head in the mass-chalice. Brigit refused the chalice. "Why," saith the ecclesiatic, "dost thou refuse it?" "Not hard to say," saith Brigit, "this is why I refuse: the head of a he-goat is shewn unto me in the chalice." The bishop called the gillie [servant] who brought the portable altar, saying, "Make thy confessions, O gillie," saith the bishop. "This very morning," saith the gillie, "I went to the goat-house, and took thereout a fat he-goat, and his flesh I ate." The gillie did penance and repented. Brigit thereafter went to the sacrament and saw not the semblance.

Once upon a time came seven bishops to Brigit, and she had nought to give them after milking the cows thrice. So the cows were milked again the third time, and it was greater than any milking.

Once upon a time a certain nun of Brigit's family took a longing for salt. Brigit made prayer, and the stone before her she turned into salt, and then the nun was cured.

Once upon a time a shepherd of Brigit's family was cutting firewood. It came to pass that he killed a pet fox of the King of Leinster's. The shepherd was seized by the King. Brigit ordered a wild fox to come out of the wood. So he came and was playing and sporting for the hosts and the King at Brigit's order. But when the fox had finished his feats he went safe back through the wood, with the hosts of Leinster behind him, both foot and horse and hound.

This was one of Brigit's miracles: She had a great band of reapers a-reaping. A rainstorm poured on the plain of Liffey, but, through Brigit's prayer, not a drop fell on her field.

This was one of Brigit's miracles: She blessed the table-faced man, so that his two eyes were whole.

This was one of Brigit's miracles: Robbers stole her oxen. The river Liffey rose against them. The oxen came home on the morrow with the robbers' clothes on their horns.

This was one of Brigit's miracles: When she came to the widow Lassair on Mag Coel, and Lassair killed her cow's calf for Brigit and burnt the beam of her loom thereunder, God so wrought for Brigit that the beam was whole on the morrow and the calf was biding along with its mother.

Once upon a time Brenainn came from the west of Ireland to Brigit, to the plain of Liffey. For he wondered at the fame that Brigit had in miracles and marvels. Brigit came from her sheep to welcome Brenainn. As Brigit entered the house she put her wet cloak on the rays of the sun, and they supported it like pot-hooks. Brenainn told his gillie to put his cloak on the same rays, and the gillie put it on them, but it fell from them twice. Brenainn himself put it, the third time, with anger and wrath, and the cloak staid upon them.

Each of them confessed to the other. Said Brenainn: "Not usual is it for me to go over seven ridges without giving my mind to God." Said Brigit: "Since I first gave my mind to God, I never took it from Him at all."

While Brigit was herding sheep, there came a thief unto her and stole seven wethers[20] from her, after having first besought her for them. Nevertheless, when the flock was counted the wethers were found again therein through Brigit's prayer.

A certain man of Brigit's family once made some mead for the King of Leinster. When the King came to consume it, not a

[20] A castrated ram.

drop thereof was found, for Brigit had given all the mead to the poor. Brigit at once rose up to protect the host, and blessed the vessels, and they were at once full of choice mead. For everything which Brigit used to ask of the Lord used to given to her at once. For this was her desire: to feed the poor, to repel every hardship, to be gentle to every misery.

Many miracles and marvels in that wise the Lord wrought for Saint Brigit. Such is their number that no one could relate them unless her own spirit, or an angel of God, should come from heaven to relate them.

Now there never hath been any one more bashful or more modest than that holy virgin. She never washed her hands, or her feet, or her head, amongst men. She never looked into a male person's face. She never spoke without blushing. She was abstinent, innocent, liberal, patient. She was joyous in God's commandments, steadfast, lowly, forgiving, charitable. She was a consecrated vessel for keeping Christ's body. She was a temple of God. Her heart and her mind were a throne of rest for the Holy Ghost. Towards God she was simple; towards the wretched she was compassionate; in miracles she was splendid. Therefore her type among created things is the dove among birds, the vine among trees, the sun above stars.

This is the father of this holy virgin—the Heavenly Father. This is her son—Jesus Christ. This is her fosterer—the Holy Ghost: and thence it is that this holy virgin wrought these great innumerable marvels.

She is it that helpeth everyone who is in straits and in danger. She it is that abateth the pestilences. She it is that quelleth the wave-voice and the wrath of the great sea. This is the prophesied woman of Christ. She is the Queen of the South. She is the Mary of the Gael.

Now when Brigit came to the ending-days, after founding churches and church buildings in plenty, after miracles and wondrous deeds in number like the sand of sea or stars of heaven, after charity and mercy, she received communion and sacrifice from Ninnid the Pure-handed, when he had returned from Rome of Latium, and sent her spirit thereafter to heaven. But her remains and her relics are on earth with great honour and with primacy and pre-eminence with miracles and marvels. Her soul is like the sun in the heavenly City among choirs of angels and archangels, in union with cherubim and seraphim, in union with Mary's Son, to wit, in the union with all the Holy Trinity, Father and Son and Holy Ghost.

I beseech the Lord's mercy, through Saint Brigit's intercession. May we all attain that union in sæcula sæculorum. Amen.

Life of Saint Brigid the Virgin
By Cogitosus

rothers, you press me to begin an account of the miracles and deeds of the virgin Brigid, of blessed memory. I am to take heed of the example of men of learning and to consult written documents as well as people's memories.

This task which you have imposed on me involves a subject difficult and delicate, and I am poorly equipped for it because of my inadequacy, my ignorance, and my lack of capacity to express myself. However, God hath the power to make much of little, as when he filled the poor widow's house from naught but a drop of oil and a handful of meal (cf. 1 Kings 17:7-16).

I must, therefore, to do as I am told with contentment, since I undertake this at your bidding. So—to avoid the fault of disobedience—I shall attempt to rescue from obscurity and ambiguity some small part of that extensive tradition which has been passed down by people who are greater and more learned than I am. In this manner may all eyes clearly see the great qualities of that virgin, who flourished in virtue. Not that my memory, nor that my meager talent and my rustic style of writing are adequate for the performance of such a great task;

but your cheerful faith and sustained prayer can help to make good the author's deficiencies.

The woman of whom I speak, then, grew in virtue, remarkably, and the fame of her good deeds attracted innumerable people of both sexes to come from every region of Ireland and gather unto her, willingly making their votive offerings. Because of this, she established a monastery—on the firm foundation of the faith—in the open expanses of the plain of Life [north County Kildare]. It is the head of virtually all the Irish churches and occupies the first place, excelling all the monasteries of the Irish. Its jurisdiction extends over the whole land of Ireland from sea to sea.

Her interest was to provide for the orderly direction of souls in all things, and she was concerned about the churches which adhered to her in many territories. Taking thought, she decided that she could not make her foundation without a high priest who could consecrate churches and confer orders on the clergy. She called on a famous hermit, distinguished in every way, a man through whom God made much goodness manifest, to leave his hermitage and his solitary life and to come and join her in that place so that he might rule the church with her in episcopal dignity, and so ensure that nothing of the priestly office would be lacking in her establishments.

And afterwards, this anointed principal of all the bishops, and Brigid, most blessed head of all the women, built their church in happy partnership, guided by virtue. Their episcopal and feminine see, like a fertile vine expanding everywhere in growing branches, spread throughout the whole island of Ireland.

She continues to rule (through a happy line of succession and a perpetual ceremonial) venerated by the archbishop of the

Irish and by the abbess [of Kildare], as well as by all the Irish abbesses. In conclusion, therefore—under pressure from the brothers, as I have said—I shall try to tell of this virgin Brigid, both what she accomplished before she came to her princely office and what were her marvelous attainments afterwards. I shall make every effort to be succinct, even though my brevity may lead to some confusion in the order in which I narrate her wonderful works.

The Life of Saint Brigid

1. Of Her Parents

The holy Brigid, whom God knew beforehand and whom he predestined to be molded in his image (cf. Rom. 8:29), was born in Ireland of noble Christian parents stemming from the good and most accomplished tribe of Eochu. Her father was Dubtach, her mother Broicsech. From her childhood she was dedicated to goodness. Chosen by God, the girl was of sober manners, modest and womanly, constantly improving her habit of life. Who could give a full account of the works she performed at an early age? From the innumerable instances I shall select a few and offer them by way of example.

2. A Miraculous Supply of Butter

In course of time, when she came of suitable age, her mother sent her to the dairy, to churn and make butter from cows' milk, so that she too would serve in the same way as the women who were accustomed to engage in this work. For a period she and the other women were left to themselves. At the end of the period, they were required to have produced a plentiful return of milk and curds, and measures of churned butter. But this beautiful maiden, with her generous nature, chose to obey God rather than men, she gave the milk to the poor and to wayfarers, and also handed out the butter.

At the end of this period the time came for all to make a return of their dairy production; and it duly came to her turn. Her co-workers could show that they had fulfilled their quota. The blessed virgin Brigid was asked if she too could present the result of her labor. She had nothing to show, having given all away to the poor, she was not allowed any extension of time, and she trembled with fear of her mother.

Burning with the fire of an inextinguishable faith, she turned to God in prayer. The Lord heard the voice of the maiden raised in prayer and responded without delay. Through the bounty of the divine will, He who is our help in adversity answered her faith in him by providing a plentiful supply of butter. Marvelous to behold, at the very moment of the maiden's prayer, not only was her quota seen to be filled, but her production was found to be much greater than that of her fellow workers. And they, seeing with their own eyes such a mighty marvel, praised the Lord, who had done this, and thought it wonderful that such faith should have its base in Brigid's virginal heart.

3. Brigid Takes the Veil

Not long afterwards, her parents, in the ordinary way of the world, wished to betroth her to a man. But heaven inspired her to decide otherwise: to present herself as a chaste virgin to God. She sought out the very holy bishop Mac Caille, of blessed memory. He was impressed by her heavenly longings, her modesty, and her virginal love of chastity, and he veiled her saintly head in a white cloth. She went down on her knees in the presence of God and the bishop, and she touched the wooden base that supported the altar. The wood retains to the present day the wonderful effect of that gesture long ago: it is as green as if the sap still flowed from the roots of a flourishing tree, and as if the tree had not long ago been felled and stripped of its bark. Even today it cures infirmities and diseases of the faithful.

4. A Marvelous Supply of Pork

It seems right not to pass over another marvel which this outstanding handmaid in the service of the Lord is purported to have worked.

Once, when she was cooking pork in the boiling trough, a dog came fawning and begging, and she gave him the food out of pity. But, when the pork was taken from the trough and divided among the guests, the amount in the trough was found to be still undiminished, for its quantity had not been reduced. Those who saw this marveled at the girl, so full of merit, so outstanding in her devotion to the faith, and they rightly spread abroad fitting praise of her wonderful works.

5. Her Crops Remain Dry in a Rainstorm

Once she gathered reapers and other workers to glean her crops, but as they assembled, a storm of rain came on the harvest. The rain poured down in torrents all over the surrounding territory, and streams of water gushed through the gulleys and ditches. Her crops alone remained dry, undisturbed by rain or storm. While all the reapers throughout the surrounding region were unable to work because of the day's downpour, her harvesters unaffected by cloud or shadow of rain, carried on their work from dawn to dusk, through the power of God.

6. A Wonderful Supply of Milk from One Cow

Among her other achievements, this one seems a cause for wonder. It so happened that some bishops were coming as her guests, and she had not the ability to feed them. But the manifold grace of God gave her abundant help when she needed it. She milked a cow three times in one day, contrary to what is normal. And the amount of milk she would normally obtain from three of the best cows, she drew on this from the one cow on this extraordinary occasion.

7. She Hangs Her Cloak on a Sunbeam

I relate here another episode which demonstrates her sanctity; one in which what her hand did corresponded to the quality of her pure virginal mind.

It happened that she was pasturing her sheep on a grassy spot on the plain when she was drenched by heavy rain, and she returned home in wet clothes. The sun shining through an aperture in the building cast a beam inside which, at a casual glance, seemed to her to be a solid wooden joist set across the house. She placed her wet cloak on it as if it were indeed solid and the cloak hung safely from the immaterial sunbeam.

When the inhabitants of the house spread the word of this great miracle among the neighbors, they extolled the incomparable Brigid with fitting praise.

8. Stolen Sheep Are Miraculously Replaced

And this next work must not be passed over in silence. St Brigid was in the fields with a flock of grazing sheep and was absorbed in her pastoral care, when a certain evil youth, who knew her reputation for giving away her charges to the poor, skillfully and surreptitiously stole and carried off seven wethers [castrated rams] in the course of one day and hid them away. But towards evening, when the flock was driven as usual to the sheepfold and was counted most carefully three or four times, marvelous to relate, the number was found to be whole and complete, without deficiency Those who were in the know were overwhelmed at the goodness of God made manifest through the maiden and returned the seven wethers to their flock. But the number in the flock was neither greater nor less than before, but was restored exactly to the original tally

The most renowned handmaid of God was, not surprisingly, famous everywhere for these and innumerable other wonders: she was seen to be worthy of the highest praise.

9. She Turns Water into Beer

On another extraordinary occasion, this venerable Brigid was asked by some lepers for beer but had none. She noticed water that had been prepared for baths. She blessed it, in the goodness of her abiding faith, and transformed it into the best beer, which she drew copiously for the thirsty. It was indeed He who turned water into wine in Cana of Galilee who turned water into beer here, through this most blessed woman's faith.

10. She Miraculously Ends a Pregnancy

When, however, this miracle is told, it provides a wonderful example.

A certain woman who had taken the vow of chastity fell, through youthful desire of pleasure, and her womb swelled with child. Brigid, exercising the most potent strength of her ineffable faith, blessed her, causing the foetus to disappear, without coming to birth, and without pain. She faithfully returned the woman to health and to penance.

11. Brigid Makes Salt from Rock

And afterwards, since all things are possible for those who believe, even things that are outside the range of ordinary everyday possibility, she performed innumerable miracles.

One day, when a certain person came asking for salt, just as other poor and destitute people in countless numbers were accustomed to come to her seeking their needs, the most blessed Brigid supplied an ample amount. She made it from a rock, which she blessed at that moment in order that she might be able to give the alms. And the suppliant went home joyfully from her, carrying the salt.

12. She Miraculously Cures Blindness

And it seems to me that this further, most divine, wonder-work of hers should be added to the list. For, following the example of the Savior, she worked in God's name a superlative marvel.

Following the Lord's example, she opened the eyes of a person who was born blind. The Lord gave His followers license to imitate His works since, as He said, "I am the light of the world" (John 8:!2), He also said to His apostles, "You are the light of the world" (Matt. 5:14), and, speaking to them, He also affirmed, "The works that I shall do they do also; and greater works than these shall they do" (John 14:12).

Brigid's faith, like the grain of mustard seed, worked on the one born blind and, just like the Lord, she produced by a great miracle eyes with normal sight. By such remarkable works, through the humility of her heart and the purity of her mind, and through her temperate ways and spiritual grace, she earned the great authority that came to her, and the fame which exalted her name above the virgins of her time.

13. She Cures a Child of Dumbness

And, on another day, a woman from outside the community came to visit, bringing along her twelve-year-old daughter, who was dumb from birth. With the great veneration and reverence that all were accustomed to show to Brigid, the woman bowed down and bent her neck to Brigid's kiss of peace. Brigid, friendly and cheerful, spoke to her in words of salvation based on divine goodness. And, following the example of the Savior, who bade the little children come to Him, she took the daughter's hand in hers and—not knowing that the child was mute—she proceeded to ask the girl's intentions, whether she wished to take the veil and remain a virgin or whether she preferred to be given in marriage. The mother intervened to point out that there would be no response, at which Brigid replied that she would not relinquish the daughter's hand until the girl had answered.

And when she put the question to the girl the second time, the daughter responded to her, saying: "I wish to do nothing but what you wish." And, after her mouth had been freed of the impediment to her speech, the girl, released from her chain of dumbness, spoke quite normally.

14. A Dog Guards Meat for Her

And this further work of hers, of which everyone has heard, who is left wholly unmoved by it?

Once, when she went into a trance, as was her custom, her soul in celestial meditation, sending up her thoughts from earth to heaven, she left down by a dog, not a small amount but a large quantity of bacon. After a month, the meat was looked for and was found just where the dog was—intact.

Not only had the dog not dared to eat what the blessed virgin had put down, but, as docile guardian of the bacon, he was tamed by divine power and was seen to act against his nature.

15. Her Mantle is Not Stained by Raw Meat

The number of her miracles grew daily, so that it is almost impossible to count them, so much did she devote herself to the duty of pity and to ministering to the poor people's need of alms, in and out of season.

For example, when a certain indigent person asked her for something from the food supply set aside for the poor, she hastened to those who cooked the meat so that she could obtain something for alms. One boorish servant among the meat-cooks slopped uncooked meat into the fold of her white garment. She carried the meat to the poor man and gave it to him, but her mantle was neither ruffled nor discolored.

16. A Cow Accepts Another Cow's Calf at Her Behest

Nor indeed is this particularly remarkable among her holy acts.

Among the poor and the strangers from every quarter who thronged to her, drawn by the reputation of her great deeds and the excess of her generosity, there came a certain wretched leper, who asked that the best cow of the herd, with the best of all the calves, be given to him. Far from spurning this request, she soon willingly gave the best possible cow from the herd, along with another cow's calf that had been chosen as the best, to this importunate afflicted person. From pity, she sent her chariot along with him, so that in his long weary journey across the wide plain he would not be troubled with concern about the cow. She directed that the calf be placed beside him in the chariot. And so the cow followed, licking the calf with her tongue as if he were her own, and attending to him, without any drover, until they reached their destination.

See, dearest brothers, how brute beasts obeyed her, even contrary to their nature.

17. A River Rises Up Against Cattle Rustlers

After some time had passed, some wicked thieves, who had regard for neither God nor man, came on a robbing expedition from a certain territory. They crossed the wide bed of a stream on foot, and they stole her cow. But, as they returned by the way they had come, a sudden flood created a great river, whose onrush overwhelmed them. That river, however, stood like a wall, and allowed the blessed Brigid's cow to cross back over it; but it bowled over the thieves and carried them along with its flood, freeing other stolen cattle from their possession.

These returned, with the thongs hanging loosely from their horns, to their proper pastures.

18. Her Chariot is Drawn by a Single Horse

See how the power of God is revealed.

One day certain business required that the most holy Brigid attend an assembly of the people. She sat in her chariot, which was drawn by two horses. As was her custom, she meditated while in her vehicle, practicing here on earth the way of life of heaven, and she prayed to her Lord. One of the horses stumbled, and the other, in the alarm of a dumb beast, sprang from the chariot and, extricating itself from the harness and from the yoke, ran away in fright across the plain.

But God's hand held up the yoke and kept it suspended without falling. Brigid sat praying in the vehicle drawn by one horse, and arrived safely at the assembly in full view of the crowd, who followed along after this display of divine power. And when she addressed the gathering with words of salvation, her teaching was reinforced by these marvels and by the signs of the divine protection she enjoyed.

19. A Wild Boar Joins Her Herd

And it seems to me that this work of hers is particularly worth considering—

Once a solitary wild boar which was being hunted ran out from the woods, and in its wild flight was brought suddenly into the most blessed Brigid's herd of swine. She observed its arrival among her pigs and blessed it. Thereupon it lost its fear and settled down among the herd. See, brothers how brute beasts and animals could withstand neither her bidding nor her wish but served her tamely and humbly.

20. Wolves Becomes Swineherds for Her

Among the many people who offered her gifts was a man who came once from a distant territory. He said that he would give her fat pigs but asked that she send some of her people with him back to his farm to collect the pigs. The farm was far away, situated at the space of three or four days' journey. She sent some of her workers with him as travelling companions, but they had in fact gone barely a day's journey (as far as the mountain known as Grabor, which forms a territorial boundary) when they saw his pigs, which they though to be in distant parts, coming towards them on the road, driven by wolves which had carried them off. As soon as he realized what had happened, the man recognized them as his pigs. Truly, the wild wolves, because of their enormous reverence for the blessed Brigid, had left the great forests and the wide plains to work at herding and protecting the pigs. Now, on the arrival of the people she had sent—who were astonished to see such swineherds—the wolves, leaving the pigs there, gave up their unnatural activity. The next day, those who had been sent to collect the pigs gave an account of the marvelous event and returned to their homes.

21. A Wild Fox Takes the Place of a King's Pet

It seems to me that this should be the last of her miraculous deeds to be passed over.

On another day, a certain person, not knowing the circumstances, saw the king's fox walking into the royal palace, and ignorantly thought it to be a wild animal. He did not know that it was a pet, familiar with the king's hall, which entertained the king and his companions with various tricks that it had learned—requiring both intelligence and nimbleness of body. He killed the fox in the view of a large crowd. Immediately, he was seized by the people who had seen the deed. He was accused and brought before the king. When the king heard the story he was angry. He ordered that, unless the man could produce a fox with all the tricks that his fox had had, he and his wife and sons should be executed, and all his household be committed to servitude.

When the venerable Brigid heard this story, she was moved to such pity and tenderness that she ordered her chariot to be yoked. Grieving in the depths of her heart for the unhappy man who had been so unjustly judged, and offering prayers to the Lord, she travelled across the plain and took the road which led to the royal palace. And the Lord, instantly, heard her out-poured prayers. He directed one of his wild foxes to come to her, it immediately made all speed, and when it arrived at the most blessed Brigid's chariot it sprang aboard and sat quietly beside Brigid under her mantle.

As soon as she arrived in the king's presence, she began imploring that unfortunate man, who had not understood the situation and was held prisoner as a victim of his own ignorance, should be set free and released from his chains. But the king would not heed her prayers. He affirmed that he would not release the man unless he could produce another fox with the same tricks as his, that had been killed. In the middle of this she introduced her fox. And, in the presence of the king and of the crowd, it went through all the tricks that the other fox had performed and amused the crowd in exactly the same way.

The king was satisfied. His nobles, and the great applauding crowd wondered at the marvel that had been worked. The king ordered that the man who had been under sentence of death should be set free. Not long after St. Brigid had procured that man's release and had returned home, the same fox, bothered by the crowds, skillfully contrived a safe escape. It was pursued by large numbers of riders and hounds, but made fools of them, fled through the plains, and went into the waste and wooded places and so to its den.

And all venerated St. Brigid, who excelled more and more in her great works. They marveled at what had been achieved through the excellence of her virtue and through the prerogative of so many gifts of grace.

22. Wild Ducks Come to Her

On another day the blessed Brigid felt a tenderness for some ducks that she saw swimming on the water and occasionally taking wing. She commanded them to come to her. And. as if they were humans under obedience, a great flock of them flew on feathered wings to her, without any fear. Having touched them with her hand and caressed them, she let them go and fly away through the air. She praised highly the Creator of all things, to whom all life is subject, and for whose service—as has been said—all life is given.

And from these examples it is plain that the whole order of beasts, flocks, and herds was subject to her rule.

23. A Band of Murderers is Deceived by a Miracle

Now this miracle of hers, one to be celebrated in all ages, must be told to the ears of the faithful.

Once, as was her custom, she was spreading abroad among everyone the seed of the Lord's word, when she observed nine men belonging to a certain peculiarly vain and diabolical cult. They were deceived and corrupted in mind and soul, and at the instigation of the ancient Enemy who ruled among them, they had bound themselves—since they thirsted for the spilling of blood— and resolved with evil vows and oaths to commit murder before the beginning of the forthcoming month of July. The most revered and kindly Brigid preached to them in many gentle phrases, urging them to abandon their mortal errors, to humble their hearts and through true penance to renounce their sinfulness. But they were profane of mind, they had not fulfilled their wicked vow, and they continued their wavs, resisting her appeal, and in spite of the abundant prayers which the virgin had poured out to God in her desire (following her Lord) that all should be saved and know the truth.

The criminals went on their way and met with what they thought was the man they had to kill. They pierced him with their spears and beheaded him with their swords and were seen by many to return with bloody weapons, as if they had destroyed their adversary. Here was the miracle: they had killed nobody—although it seemed to them that they had fulfilled their vows. When, however, no person was missing in that territory in which they thought they had triumphed, the fulness of the divine favor granted through the most holy Brigid became known to all. And they who had formerly been murderers were now turned back to God through penance.

24. Brigid Cures a Man of Overeating

Words cannot adequately describe St. Brigid's devotion to God, through which the divine power of holy religion was shown in the following work.

There was a certain man called Luguidam, a strong man for sure, and one of the bravest. When he was of a mind, he did the work of twelve men in a single day all by himself. At the same time, he ate enough food to feed twelve men (as he could do the work singlehanded, so could he consume the rations). He implored Brigid to pray to almighty God to moderate his appetite, which caused him to eat to such excess, but he asked that he should not lose his former strength along with his appetite. Brigid blessed him and prayed to God for him. Afterwards, he was content with the sustenance of one man, but, just as before, when he worked he could do the labor of twelve. He had all his former strength.

25. The Miraculous Movement of a Huge Tree

Among all her famous works we should recount the following to all—one which is extraordinary and is well verified.

A huge and magnificent tree, which was to be used for certain purposes, was cut down and trimmed with axes by skillful craftsmen. Its great size caused such difficulty in maneuvering it that a gathering of strong men was summoned to transport the tree with its awkward branches through difficult places. Aided by the craftsmen's tackle, they proposed to haul it with many oxen to the place where it was to be dealt with. But in spite of the large number of men, the strength of the oxen, and the skill of the craftsmen, they were unable to budge the tree; so they drew back from it.

But the Master teaches through the medium of the heavenly Gospel that it is possible for faith to move mountains; and—through Brigid's stalwart faith (like the grain of mustard seed)—they carried this weightiest of trees without the slightest difficulty, through the divine mystery of the power of the Gospel and without any mortal aid, to the place designated by St. Brigid. This display of the excellence of God's power was made known through all the territories.

26. She Vindicates a Woman Accused of Theft

And it comes to mind that we should not omit the following manifestation of divine power, which, among innumerable other miracles, was worked by the venerable Brigid.

There was a certain nobleman, with the deviousness of a man of the world, who lusted after a particular woman. He exercised his cunning on ways to seduce her. He entrusted a silver brooch to her safe keeping, then deviously filched it from her without her knowledge and threw it into the sea. This meant that, when she was unable to produce it on demand, she would be forfeit to him as his slave, and so must submit to his embraces to be used as he wished. He contrived this evil for no other reason than to be in a position to demand this ransom. If the silver brooch were not returned, the woman herself must be given to him instead in servitude, because of her failure, to be subject to his wicked lust.

This chaste woman fled in fear to St Brigid, as she would fly to the safest city of refuge. When Brigid learned what had happened, and how and why; almost before she had heard the story out she summoned a certain person who had fish that had been caught in the river. The fishes' bellies were cut and opened, and there in the middle of one of them was revealed the silver brooch which that most cruel man had thrown into the sea.

Then, easy in her mind, she took along the silver brooch and went with that infamous man to the assembly of the people for the case to be heard. She showed the assembly the brooch, and many witnesses gave testimony, people who were able to identify the brooch as the same one that was concerned in this accusation. Brigid took the chaste woman into her own company and freed her from the clutches of that most cruel tyrant. Indeed, he afterwards confessed his fault to St. Brigid and submissively prostrated himself before her. Everyone admired her for the performance of this great miracle, and she gave thanks to God (for whose glory she had done everything) and went home.

27. She Miraculously Replaces a Calf and a Loom

In the telling of these wonders, we may compare to her hospitality that of another woman.

For St. Brigid came to her dwelling while making a journey on God's business across the wide plain of Brega [mainly in Co. Meath). She arrived as the day was declining into evening, and she spent the night with this woman, who received her joyfully with outstretched hands and gave thanks to God for the happy arrival of the most revered Brigid, Christ's virgin. The woman was too poor to have ready the wherewithal to entertain such guests, but she broke up the loom on which she had been weaving cloth, for firewood. Then she killed her calf, placed it on the heap of kindling and, with a good will, lit the fire. Dinner was eaten, and the night was passed with the customary vigils.

The hostess (who had taken the calf from her cow in order that nothing should be lacking in the reception and entertainment of St Brigid) rose early. The cow had discovered another calf, in the same form exactly as the calf she had previously loved. And a loom was to be seen, exactly in the same shape and form as the other.

So, having accomplished this marvel, and having bidden farewell to the people of the house, St. Brigid continued on her pontifical way and went cheerfully on her journey.

28. She Divides a Silver Dish Exactly into Three

Her miracles are great, but this one is especially admired.

Three lepers came, asking for alms of any kind, and she gave them a silver dish. So that this would not cause discord and contention among them when they came to share it out, she spoke to a certain person expert in weighing of gold and silver and asked him to divide it among them in three parts of equal weight. When he began to excuse himself, pointing that there was no way he could divide it up so that the three parts would be exactly the same, the most blessed Brigid herself took the silver dish and struck it against a stone, breaking it into three parts as she had wished. Marvelous to tell, when the three parts were tested on the scales, not one was found to be heavier or lighter by a breath than any other. So the three poor people left with their gift and there was no cause for envy or grudging between them.

29. She Receives a Bishop's Vestments from Christ

She followed the example of the most blessed Job and never allowed a poor person to leave empty-handed. Indeed, she gave away to the poor the foreign and exotic robes of the illustrious bishop Conlaeth, vestments wore in the course of the liturgy of the Lord and the apostolic vigils.

When in due course the time for these solemnities came round, the high priest of the people wished to change into his vestments. It was to Christ—in the form of a poor person—that St Brigid had given the bishop's clothing. Now she handed the bishop another set of vestments, similar in all details of texture and color, which she had received at that very moment (draped over a two-wheeled chariot) from Christ, whom, as a beggar, she had clad. She had freely given the other clothes to the poor. Now, at the right moment, she received these instead. For, as she was the living and most blessed instrument of the sublime, she had power to do what she wished.

30. She Divines a Supply of Honey

After this, a certain man, finding himself in particular need, came to her to ask for a sixth of a measure of honey. She was distressed in her mind, because she had no honey ready that she might give to the person who was asking for it, when the humming of bees was heard underneath the paved floor of the building in which she was. And when that spot from which the buzzing of the bees was heard, was excavated and examined, there was found a sufficient quantity to meet the man's requirements. And he, receiving the gift of enough honey for his needs, returned joyfully to his village.

31. She Miraculously Diverts a River

In the following episode, too, she performed a miracle. The king of her country (the region in which she lived) issued a decree for all the tribes and places under his rule. All the people were to come together from his territories to build a wide road. It was to be solidified with tree branches and stones in the foundation, it was to have very strong banks and deep impassable ditches, and it was to run through soggy ground and through a swamp in which a full river flowed. When built it should be able to carry four-wheeled cars, horsemen, chariots, wagon-wheels, and the traffic of people as well as that of forces to assault enemies on all sides.

When the people had gathered in from every quarter, they divided up the road they had to build into sections, by septs and families, so that each tribe or family would build the section assigned to it. The most difficult and laborious section was that with the river, and it was assigned to a certain tribe. These people decided to avoid the heavy work, so they used their strength to force a weaker tribe (that to which St. Brigid belonged) to labor on the difficult section. Choosing an easier section for themselves, this cruel tribe could do their construction without facing the hazard of the river.

St. Brigid's own blood-relations came and prostrated themselves at her feet. It is reliably reported that she told them, "Go. God has the will and the power to move the river from the location where you are oppressed by hard labor to the section that they have chosen." And, when at the dawn of that day the people rose to work, the river which had been complained of was found to have left its former valley and the two banks between which it had flowed. It had transferred from the section in which St Brigid's tribe had been forced to labor to the section of those powerful and proud people who had unjustly compelled the smaller and weaker tribe to work there. In proof of the miracle, the traces of the river which transferred to a different place, and the empty channel through which it flowed in past time; these may still be seen, dry and without any trickle of water.

32. She Continues Working Miracles After Death

Many miracles were performed in her lifetime, before she laid down the burden of her flesh, and many later. The bounty of the gift of God never ceased working wonders in her monastery, where her venerable body lies. We have not only heard tell of these marvels; we have seen them with our own eyes.

33. A Millstone is Miraculously Brought to the Mill

For example, the prior of the great and famous monastery of St. Brigid (of the beginnings of which we have made brief mention in this little work) sent masons and stonecutters to look in suitable places for a rock fit for making a millstone. They made no provision for transport, but went up a steep and difficult road, reached the top of a rocky mountain and chose a great stone at the summit of the tallest peak. And they carved it all over to a round shape and perforated it to make a millstone. When the prior arrived, in response to their message, with an ox-team, he was unable to drive the oxen up to pull the stone; he was barely able to ascend the very difficult track with a few of them following him.

He and all his workers pondered this problem: by what means could remove the millstone from the highest ridge of the mountain when there was no way in which the oxen could be yoked and burdened in that high and precipitous place? They came to the despairing conclusion (some of them even giving up and descending the mountain) that they should abandon the stone and regard as waste the labor they had put into fashioning it. The prior, however, taking prudent thought and consulting his workers, said confidently: "By no means let it be so; but manfully lift this millstone and cast it down from the high peak of the mountain in the name—and calling on the power—of the most revered St. Brigid. For we have neither equipment nor strength to move the millstone through this rocky place, unless Brigid, to whom nothing is impossible (all things are possible to the believer), will carry it to a place from which the oxen can pull it." So, with firm faith, they first gradually raised it from the mountain top and then cast it into the valley. When they flung it down, it found its way; sometimes avoiding rocks, sometimes springing over them, rolling through damp places high on the mountain in which neither men nor cattle could stand, and, with marvelous noise, it arrived quite unbroken at the level spot where the oxen were. From there it was transported by the ox-team as far as the millhouse, where it was skillfully matched with the other stone.

34. The Millstone Refuses to Grind a Druid's Corn

There is another, previously untold but quite outstanding, miracle to add the story (now known to everyone) of the millstone that was moved in the name of St. Brigid. A certain pagan, living near the millhouse, sent some grain from his house to the mill, employing a simple and ignorant man so that the miller who did the work there did not know that the grain was his. And when that grain was spread between the millstones, nothing could budge them—not the power of the water, and no exercise of strength or skill. When the people who observed this sought its cause, they were quite perplexed.

Then, when they learned that the grain belonged to a druid, they had no doubt at all that the millstone upon which St. Brigid had performed the divine miracle had refused to grind the pagan man's grain into flour. And immediately they removed the heathen's grain and placed their own grain, from the monastery, under the millstone. Straightaway the mill machinery resumed its normal course without any impediment.

35. The Millstone Remains Intact in a Fire

And after an interval of time it happened that this very millhouse caught fire. It was no small miracle that, when the fire consumed the whole building, including the other stone which was matched to St. Brigid's millstone, the flames did not dare to touch or scorch her stone. It remained unaffected by the fire in the conflagration that destroyed the millhouse.

And afterwards, since note was taken of this miracle, the stone was brought to the monastery and placed near the gate, inside the cashel that encloses the church where many come to venerate St. Brigid. It was given a place of honor in that gate, and it cures diseases of the faithful who touch it.

36. The Miraculously Rebuilt Door

Nor must one be silent about the miracle of the rebuilding of the church in which the bodies of that glorious pair, the bishop Conleth and this holy virgin Brigid, lie right and left of the ornamented altar, placed in shrines decorated with a variegation of gold, silver, gems and precious stones, with gold and silver crowns hanging above them.

In fact, to accommodate the increasing number of the faithful, of both sexes, the church is spacious in its floor area, and it rises to an extreme height. It is adorned with painted boards and has on the inside three wide chapels, all under the roof of the large building and separated by wooden partitions. One partition, which is decorated with painted images and is covered with linen, stretches transversely in the eastern part of the church from one wall to the other and has two entrances, at its ends. By one entrance, placed in the external part, the supreme pontiff enters the sanctuary and approaches the altar with his retinue of monks. To these consecrated ministers are entrusted the sacred vessels for Sunday use and the offering of the sacrifice. And by the other entrance, placed on the left side of the above-mentioned transverse partition, the abbess, with her faithful virgins and widows, equally enters to enjoy the banquet of the body and blood of Jesus Christ.

And another partition, dividing the floor of the church into two equal parts, extends from the cast in length as far as the transverse wall. The church has many windows, and an ornamented door on the right side through which the priests and the faithful of male sex enter the building. There is another door on the left through which the virgins and the congregation of the female faithful are accustomed to enter. And so, in one great basilica, a large number of people, arranged by rank and sex, in orderly division separated by partitions, offers prayers with a single spirit to the almighty Lord.

When the ancient door of the left-hand entrance, through which St. Brigid was accustomed to enter the church, was set on its hinges by the craftsmen, it did not fill the new entrance of the rebuilt church. In fact, a quarter of the opening was left unclosed and agape. If a fourth part, by height, were added, then the door could be restored to fit the opening. The artificers deliberated and discussed whether they should make a completely new, and larger, door which would fill the opening, or whether they should make a timber piece to attach to the old door, to bring it to the required size. The gifted master, who was in all these matters the leading craftsman of the Irish, gave wise advice. "We ought"—he said, "in this coming night, alongside St. Brigid, to pray faithfully to the Lord so that she may indicate in the morning what we should do." And so he spent the whole night praying before St. Brigid's shrine.

And, having sent on his prayer, he rose in the morning and brought the old door and placed it on its hinges. It closed the opening completely. There was no gap, no overlap. And so St. Brigid extended the height of the door so that it filled the opening, and no aperture could be seen except when the door was pushed back to allow entry to the church. And this miracle of the Lord's power is plain to the eyes of all who see this doorway and door.

37. Brigid's City

But who could convey in words the supreme beauty of her church and the countless wonders of her city, of which we would speak? "City" is the right word for it: that so many people are living there justifies the title. It is a great metropolis, within whose outskirts—which St. Brigid marked out with a clearly defined boundary—no earthly adversary is feared, nor any incursion of enemies. For the city is the safest place of refuge among all the towns of the whole land of the Irish, with all their fugitives. It is a place where the treasures of kings are looked after, and it is reckoned to be supreme in good order.

And who could number the varied crowds and countless people who gather in from all territories? Some come for the abundance of festivals; others come to watch the crowds go by; others come with great gifts to the celebration of the birth into heaven of St. Brigid who, on the First of February, falling asleep, safely laid down the burden of her flesh and followed the Lamb of God into the heavenly mansions.

Epilogue

I beg the indulgence of the brothers and of readers of these episodes since I had no pretension to knowledge but was compelled by obedience to skim over the great sea of St. Brigid's wonderful works—something to be feared by the bravest—and to offer in rustic language these few narratives of the greatest miracles.

Pray for me Cogitosus Ua hAedha, who am worthy of blame. I urge you to commend me to the good Lord in your prayers; and may God grant you the peace of the Gospel.

Here ends the life of St Brigid the virgin.

Ultan's Hymn

Brigit, excellent woman, a flame golden, delightful,
May she, the sun dazzling splendid, bear us to the eternal
    kingdom!
May Brigit save us beyond throngs of demons!
May she overthrow before us the battles of every disease!
May she destroy within us our flesh's taxes
The branch with blossoms, the mother of Jesus!
The true virgin, dear, with vast dignity:
May I be safe always, with my saint of the Lagenians![21]
One of the pillars of the Kingdom with Patrick the
    pre-eminent,
The vesture over *liga*, the Queen of Queens!
Let our bodies after old age be in sackcloth
With her grace may Brigit rain on us, save us.

---

[21] *Laighin*, the people of Leinster

Broccán's Hymn

Victorious Brigit loved not the world; she sat
the seat of John on a cliff:
she slept the sleep of a captive—
the saint, for the sake of her Son.

Not much of evil speaking was got!
with lofty faith in (the) Trinity
Brigit, mother of my high King,
of the kingdom of heaven best was she born

She was not absent, she was not malicious
she was not a mighty, quarrelsome champion (?)
she was not an adder striking, speckled;
she sold not the son of God for gain!

She was not greedy of treasures,
she gave without poison, without abatement;
she was not hard or penurious;
she loved not the world's spending.

To guests she was not acrimonious
to miserable weaklings (lepers?) she was gentle;

on a plain she built a city;
may she protect us (in) hosts to the Kingdom

She was not a plunderer on a mountain slope;
she worked in the midst of a plain,
a wonderful ladder for pagan-folk
to visit the kingdom of Mary's Son.

Wonderful St. Brigit's congregation,
wonderful, the Plea to which it went
but alone with Christ was maintained
her frequent mission to the poor.

Good was the hour that Mac-Caille held
a veil over Saint Brigit's head;
she was clear in all her proceedings;
in heaven was heard her prayer;

"God, I pray Him against every battle,
in whatever way my lips can reach,
deeper than seas, vaster than count,
Three-Persons, One-Person, a wonder of a story!"

A challenge to the battle, renowned Kevin
through a storm of snow that wind drives,
in Glendalough was suffered a cross,
till peace visited him after labor.

St. Brigid was not given to sleep,
nor was she intermittent about God's love,

not merely that she did not buy, she did not strive for
the world's wealth here below, the Saint!

That which the King wrought
of miracles for Saint Brigid,
if they have been wrought for any other person
in what place hath ear of any living being heard of it?

The first dairying on which she was sent
with first butter in a cart,
she took naught from the gift to her guests,
nor did she lessen her following.

Her portion of bacon after that,
one evening—the victory was high—
not merely was the dog satisfied with it,
the company was not grieved.

A day of reaping for her—it was well reaped,
no fault was found there with my pious one;
it was dry weather ever in her field
through the world it poured heavy rain.

Bishops visited her,
not slight was the danger to her,
if there had not been—the King helped—
milking of the cows thrice

On a day of heavy rain she herded
sheep in the midst of a plain;

she spread her upper garment afterwards
indoors across a sunbeam.

The cunning youth asked alms of her,
Brigid, for the love of her King:
She gave away seven wethers
But it did not lessen her flock's number.

It is of my poetic gift if I were to recount
what she did of good:
wonderful for her was the bath
that was blessed about her—it became red ale!

She blessed the pregnant nun,
who thereon became whole, without poison,
    without disease;
greater than others was the marvel, how
of the stone she made salt.

I record not, I enumerate not
all that the holy creature did:
she blessed the flat-faced one,
and his two eyes became quite apparent.

Someone brought a dumb girl
to Brigid—the miracle of it was unique—
whose hand went not out of her hand
till her utterances were clear.

Another wonder was bacon that she blessed;
and God's power kept it safely;

though it was a full month with the dog,
the dog did not injure it.

It was a miracle greater than others:
a morsel she requested of the kitchen-folk
did not spoil the color of her scapular[22]
though it was flung, boiling, into her bosom.

The leper begged a boon of her;
it was good boon that befell him:
she blessed the choicest of the calves
and the choicest of the cows loved it.

He directed her chariot afterwards
northward to Bri Cobthaig Coil,
the calf being with the leper in the car,
and the cow following behind the calf.

The oxen, when thieves visited them,
would have been pleased that anyone should
    hear them:
against them rose up a river,
at morn they returned home.

Her horse separated head from bridle
when they went down the slope;
the yoke was not flung out of balance
God's Son directed the royal hand.

---

[22] Meaning her habit.

A wild boar frequented her herd,
to the north he hunted the wild pig;
Brigid blessed him with her staff,
And he took up his stay with her swine.

A hog, a fat pig to her was given her,
beyond Magh Fea; it was wonderful how
wild dogs hunted it for her
till it was close to her in Uachtar-gabra.

She gave the wild fox
on behalf of her peasant, the wretched;
grace of her vassal the wretched:
to a wood it escaped
though the hosts hunted it.

She was open in her proceedings,
she was One-Mother of the Great King's Son:
she blessed the fluttering bird
so that she played with it in her hand.

Nine outlaws whose weapons she blessed
reddened those weapons in a pool of blood:
the man whom they had ill-treated
was wounded, but no hurt to him was found!

What she wrought of miracles
there is no one who could enumerate aright:
wonderful how she took away Lugaid's appetite;
but the champion's strength she did not lessen.

An oak the multitude lifted not,
on another occasion—excellent and famous deed!
her Son brought to her on the prayer of Brigid
to the place where she wished it to be (?)

The trinket of silver, which should not have
     been hidden
for mischief to the champion's handmaid
was flung into the sea the length of a mighty cast—
but even was it fund, in the inner part of a salmon.

Another wonder of hers was the widow
who refreshed her in Mag Coil,
for she made firewood of the new weaving beam,
and that for cooking the calf;

A miracle greater than any other
which the saint effected—
in the morning the beam was made whole,
with its mother was the missing calf.

The trinket of silver, which the smith
broke not—this was one of her miracles—
Brigid struck it against her hand
afterwards, so that it broke into three parts.

It was flung into the scale at the smith's;
thereupon was found a wonder:
it was not discovered that by one scruple
any third was greater than another.

What she wrought of miracles,
there is no man who may come at them;
she blessed raiment for Condlaed [Conleth]
when he was taken to Letha (?)

When she—it was a danger for her—
her Son before her failed her not (?):
he put raiment in the basket
of Roncend in a chariot of two wheels.

The mead-vat that was brought to her;
whoever brought it was not unrewarded:
for there was found honey in the wall of a house:
it had not been found there up to that!

She gave for behoof of her servant
when he stood in need;
not merely was no surplus found there,
but not a drop was wanting.

Upon us may Brigid's prayers rest!
and she against danger be our aid!
may they be on her weakling's side
before going into the presence of the Holy Spirit!

May she aid us with a sword of fire
in the fight against black swarms!
May her holy prayers protect us
past pains, into the kingdom of Heaven!

Broccán's Hymn

Before going with angels to the battle,
let us reach the church with a run!
Commemoration of the Lord is better than any poem—
victorious Brigit loved not the world.

I beseech the patronage of Saint Brigid
with the saints of Kildare:
may they be between me and pain!
may my soul not be lost!

The Nun that drove over the Curragh,
may she be a shield against the edges of sharpness!
I have not found her like, save Mary:
we honor my Brigid.

We honor my Brigid;
May she be a protection to our company!
May her patronage assist me!
May we all of us deserve escape!

Christ's praise, a glorious utterance,
adoration of the Son of God, guarantee of victory,
may it be without denial of God's kingdom,
Whoever recites it, whoever has heard it.

Whoever has heard, whoever recites it,
may the benediction of Brigid rest on him!
The benediction of Brigid and of God
rest upon us, together!

There are two nuns in the Kingdom—
I implore their aid with all my effort—
Mary and St. Brigid
under the protection of them both may we be!

Appendix:
Brigid The Pagan Goddess?

t has become lamentably common to state, as a matter of fact, that St. Brigid is a transmogrified Celtic goddess. One need only spend ten minutes searching online for articles about Brigid of Kildare to run across variants of the theory. The alleged pagan origin of St. Brigid's cult has been repeated so frequently that even otherwise scholarly publications take it to be historically factual.

Readers may then be surprised to learn that not only is the theory contested, but that it is entirely unfounded. Seeing justification in a 12th century anti-Irish tract of Gerald of Wales, scholars of the Victorian era—eager to find remnants of ancient pagandom beneath every stone—created the theory on evidence so slight that no serious historian today would propose it. The theory was given further prominence by modern neo-pagans anxious to retain devotion to St. Brigid while stripping her of everything distinctively Catholic. This has given rise to all manner of wild associations that can best be described as elaborate religio-historical fanfiction.

The theory that Brigid's cultus was originally pagan rests on six pillars: (1) The ancient Celts worshiped a fire goddess named Brigit (2) The existence of a pre-Christian cultic center at Kildare (3) Identifying the oaks of Kildare as an ancient druidic grove (4) The perpetual fire of Kildare as a survival of pagan rites to the fire goddess (5) The correspondence of Brigid's feast day (February 1) with the Celtic holiday of Imbolc (6) Alleged similarities between Brigid's *vitae* and episodes from Celtic myth.

To understand the ridiculousness of identifying St. Brigid with a Celtic goddess, we must review the merits of each of these six points.

1. Was there a Celtic fire goddess name Brigit?

One of the most surprising things newcomers to ancient Irish history learn is that the pre-Christian Gaels did not commit anything to writing. The only writing possessed by the ancient Irish was a cumbersome epigraphic script known as *ogham* which appears solely as carvings on boundary stones. It was not until the coming of Christianity that there was any manuscript tradition in Ireland. Almost all we know of the ancient Celtic mythology—whether of their gods, legends, or rituals—comes to us through the pens of Christian monks writing centuries after Irish paganism had already disappeared. That being the case, where and when do we first hear of a Celtic fire goddess name Bríg or Brigit?

The first appearance of the name at all outside of reference to the saint of Kildare is in the law tracts of the Ulster Cycle, dating from c. 700. A character named Bríg shows up as a kinswoman of the druid Sencha mac Ailella.[23] There is no

---

[23] Her relation is uncertain; she may be a wife, or mother. See Kaarina Hollo, "The Ulster Cycle, the Law-tracts, and the Medieval Court: The

indication that this Bríg is a goddess at all, and she shares no traits with St. Brigid; she is merely the human wife of the druid Sencha. There is nothing to equate her with Brigid whatsoever.

The next appearance of the name comes from the 10th century *Sanas Chormaic* ("Cormac's Glossary"). The *Sanas Chormaic*, composed around 908 by Cormac of Munster, is a glossary of important persons and terms from early Irish literature. It provides definitions and etymologies of over 1,400 Irish words, many of them obscure or outdated by Cormac's time. The *Sanas Chormaic* contains two entries for "Brigit," one for the saint of Kildare, and the other for what is said to have been a "goddess worshiped by the poets." The entry goes on to say that this Brigit had two sisters of the same name, goddess of smithcraft and healing respectively. Her name, moreover, was said to be derived from *bri-sagit*, "fiery arrow." This entry in the *Sanas Chormaic* provided the seed of the idea that Brigit was a triple goddess of fire. It is also the sole reference to a Celtic goddess by this name in any old Irish text.

Given that the *Sanas Chormaic* was composed around 908, we must first note that a goddess named Brigit is not attested until roughly 383 years *after* the historical Brigid died. Perhaps the *Sanas Chormaic* reflects beliefs from a much earlier period, but it is just as likely that it represents, not paganism as it existed in the 5th century, but paganism as 10th century Christian authors imagined it may have looked. By Cormac's time, pagan symbols and early Irish concepts were no longer comprehensible to Christian authors, at least in their original context. There is no proof outside of the *Sanas Chormaic* that

Depiction of Senchae mac Ailella, Aurlabraid Ulad," *Aiste* 1 (2007), pp. 170-180 any deity named Brigit ever existed. The goddess may be a purely literary reconstruction, similar to the Anglo-Saxon Eostre, an alleged goddess who is attested only in the writings of the Christian monk Bede and nowhere else. At any rate, it is difficult to see how the cultus of St. Brigid could have developed out of a pagan deity that is not attested until four centuries after her own life.

Furthermore, the associations the *Sanas Chormaic* attributes to this Brigit—poetry, smithcraft, and healing—bear no resemblance to the historical Brigid. None of her *vitae* suggest she was a poet or had interest in smithing; she performed many miracles but was not particularly renowned as a healer; most of her miracles concern animals or agricultural matters. Had this goddess Brigit, for example, been an agricultural goddess or a goddess of cows or something similar, we could grant a connection. But, given the lack of similarity between the character of St. Brigid and the description of this goddess in the *Sanas Chormaic*, by what logic do we assume the latter is derived from the former?

2. Was Kildare a Pre-Christian Cultic Center?

Given that almost nothing is known of the goddess Brigit (if she existed), even less is known about any cultic center at Kildare. The existence of such a pre-Christian cultic center is pure speculation. The fact is no one has excavated beneath the church of Kildare to look for any pre-Christian structures. To date, there is zero evidence, textual or archaeological, that any pagan shrine existed at Kildare. All historical evidence affirms that the site was uninhabited before Brigid founded her church.

3. Were the "Oaks of Kildare" a Druidic Grove?

The existence of a pre-Christian pagan cult at Kildare is generally inferred from toponymy—the name "Kildare" (*Cell-dara*) meaning "church of the oak." As the Celtic druids preferred forest groves for their ritual spaces, it is simply assumed that the "oak" referenced in the name Kildare must refer to an oak grove previously used in pagan worship. Thus, when St. Brigid founded her church "beneath the oak," she was quite intentionally appropriating a pagan worship site. This theory was another liberty of the Victorian era, whose writers could not resist drawing clear, definitive lines from current institutions back through time to the mists of pagan antiquity.

There is no evidence, written or archaeological, that Kildare was ever the site of a druidic grove. The name "Kildare" likely has a more mundane meaning: *Cell-dara*, commonly rendered "church of the oak," could just as easily mean "oaken church," referring to the building materials.

This is hinted at in the *Leabhar Breac*: Brigid, accompanied by the bishop St. Ibar mac Lugna, came to the Plain of Liffey with the intent of founding her church:

> ...they came thereafter to the place where Kildare is today. That was the season and the time that Ailill son of Dunlaing, with *a hundred horse-loads of peeled rods,* chanced to be going through the ground of Kildare. Two girls came from Brigit to ask for some of the rods, and they got a refusal. Forthwith all the horses were struck down under their loads against the ground. Stakes and wattles were taken from

them, and they arose not until Ailill son of Dunlaing had offered unto Brigit those one hundred horse-loads; *and thereout was built Saint Brigit's house in Kildare.*

Though the text does not say these hundred horse-loads of peeled rods were oak, it is a reasonable inference. Besides relating a miracle story, this portion of the *Leabhar Breac* is meant to explain what Kildare was built out of and why. Presumably, the construction of the original structure out of a hundred-cart loads of oaken rods was somewhat of a novelty, causing it to be nicknamed *Cell-dara*, "the oaken church."

This theory is admittedly speculative, but it has more evidence behind it than the druidic grove hypothesis.

4. Did Kildare Feature a Perpetual Fire Dating to Pagan Times?

It is often stated that medieval Kildare was the site of a perpetual flame. This flame, tended by Brigid's nuns, dated back to pagan times, and was forbidden for men to approach, being blocked by a magical hedge; men who crossed its sacred precincts were struck dead or afflicted with madness. The theory is that this sacred flame (presumably sacred to the fire goddess Brigit?) was tended by druidic priestess in pagan times. With the coming of Christianity, the site gradually transformed into a Christian center, but preserved the sacred fire. Meanwhile, Brigit the goddess had her identity reworked to become Brigid the saint.

The perpetual flame of Kildare is first mentioned in the *Topographia Hiberniae* ("Topography of Ireland") by the Norman archdeacon Gerald of Wales around 1188. The book was written in the wake of the Norman conquest of Ireland and was one of the most influential work on Ireland that circulated during the Middle Ages. The *Topographia* contains several chapters on Kildare, two of which deal with a perpetual fire. The passages are worth citing in full:

> At Kildare, in Leinster, celebrated for the glorious Brigit, many miracles have been wrought worthy of memory. Among these, the first that occurs is the fire of St. Brigit, which is reported never to go out. Not that it cannot be extinguished, but the nuns and holy women tend and feed it, adding fuel, with such watchful and diligent care, that from the time of the Virgin, it has continued burning through a long course of years; and although such heaps of wood have been consumed during this long period, there has been no accumulation of ashes.
>
> As in the time of St. Brigit twenty nuns were here engaged in the Lord's warfare, she herself being the twentieth, after her glorious departure, nineteen have always formed the society, the number having never been increased. Each of them has the care of the fire for a single night in turn, and, on the evening before the twentieth night, the last nun, having heaped wood upon the fire, says, "Brigit, take charge of your own fire; for this night belongs to you." She then leaves the fire, and in the morning it is found that the

fire has not gone out, and that the usual quantity of fuel has been used.

This fire is surrounded by a hedge, made of stakes and brushwood, and forming a circle, within which no male can enter; and if anyone should presume to enter it, which has been sometimes attempted by rash men, he will not escape the divine vengeance. Moreover, it is only lawful for women to blow the fire, fanning it or using bellows only, and not with their breath.[24]

Notice that Gerald does not assert the fire goes back to pagan times, only that it had been burning "from the time of the Virgin." Thus, the pagan connection is read into Gerald's account, not deduced from it.

There is no doubt Gerald was writing about an actually existing fire, as other contemporary sources also mention the perpetual flame at Kildare. Documents up until the late 14th century reference the fire; a 1397 roll references a "fyre house" at the church. Even today, visitors to Kildare are shown the foundations of a rectangular structure that is called "the firehouse," which tour guides identify as the site of Brigid's perpetual flame.

Nobody knows what this structure was or what it was used for; "firehouse" is simply a popular nickname. It certainly does not date from pre-Christian times; its masonry and appearance suggest it comes rather from the 10th-11th centuries. As to the

---

[24] *Giraldus Cambrensis: The Topography of Ireland,* Chap. 24-26, trans. Thomas Forester (In Parentheses Publications: Cambridge, Ontario, 2000), pp. 53-54

assertion that an ancient fire was kept burning from the time of Brigid, we shall here defer to Christina Harrington, whose scholarly work *Women in the Celtic Church* argues strongly against the existence of any such perpetual flame:

> [Regarding] the supposed perpetual flame at Kildare, the alleged sign of surviving fire worship or vestal devotion. There is no mention of it in any of the three early Lives of Brigit, namely the *Vita I,* Cogitosus, or the ninth-century *Bethu Brigte.* It is hard to imagine that it could be overlooked in all three Lives. It is, in fact, absent from all other Lives, from annals, from the martyrologies and their glosses—all sources, in fact, until Gerald of Wales, a visitor in the twelfth century, almost 700 years after the alleged pagan-Christian transition took place.[25]

If, in fact, this alleged fire ritual was so central to the cultus of Brigid at Kildare, why is it not mentioned anywhere in the 700 years prior to Gerald? We should not naively accept Gerald's assertion in the absence of any other corroborating evidence. Elsewhere in the same work, Gerald also alleges the existence of a falcon in his day that had been alive since the time of Brigid.[26]

---

[25] Christina Harrington, *Women in a Celtic Church: Ireland 450-1150* (Oxford University Press: Oxford, 2002), pp 64-65.

[26] *Topography of Ireland,* 55

Gerald also wrote with a deep anti-Irish bias. The *Topographia* was written as a propaganda piece to justify the Norman conquest. To this end, he sought to portray the Irish as half-Christianized savages still mired in the darkness of paganism. The *Topographia* contains chapters entitled "How the Irish are very ignorant in the rudiments of faith," "Of their abominable treachery," and "Proof of their wickedness." In Chapter 19, we read that the Irishman is "indeed a most filthy race, a race sunk in vice, a race more ignorant than all other nations of the first principles of faith." Gerard frequently resorts to gossip and rumormongering to argue the Irish faith is barely discernible as Christian. His analysis is hardly objective.

But what of the fire that was present in the 12th century and later? What was it? Was it the remains of some vestal pagan ritual? Again, let us return to Harrington, who says:

> Gerald did say that only nuns were allowed to tend the fire, and this may have been the case, but Kildare did have monks and clerics on its premises in his day, as in earlier centuries. Nor was the presence of a perpetual fire unique to Kildare: in the twelfth and thirteenth centuries seven others are mentioned in the hagiography, all of them at male monasteries. The inescapable conclusion is that such flames in Ireland were not especially associated with women and appear rather late in the historical record. The reasons for their existence were probably Christo-theological: the luminary imagery of Christian deity was as ubiquitous in

Ireland as it was elsewhere in the West. Why they appeared suddenly in the twelfth century is a question not ventured here.[27]

The final nail in the coffin is the fact that there is no evidence the druids had "priestesses" or any female branch. It was an exclusively male order, making it nigh on impossible that the nuns who tended the fire at Kildare were heirs to an order of ancient pagan priestesses.

5. Does Brigid's Feast Day Correspond to Imbolc?

Brigid's feast day is February 1, which is the date of the Celtic holy day of Imbolc. The very existence of the feast of Imbolc, however, is questionable. What do we truly know of this holiday?

The earliest reference to Imbolc also comes from the *Sanas Chormaic*, whose entry merely says, "the time the sheep's milk comes." Later in the 10th century, the tale *Tochmach Emire* says Imbolc is "when the ewes are milked at spring's beginning." Beyond this, little is known of Imbolc, neither how it was observed nor what gods—if any—it commemorated. Imbolc appears to have been centered on milking, and Brigid certainly was known for working with dairy animals. But this was a job all women did in ancient Ireland; there is nothing about Imbolc that connects it to Brigid specifically. Furthermore, if Brigid was a fire goddess, shouldn't she have been commemorated at Beltane, the spring fire festival? Professor Ronald Hutton, in his study of the Celtic seasonal cycle, says of Imbolc:

---

[27] Harrington, 65

The festival must be pre-Christian in origin, but there is absolutely no direct testimony as to its early nature, or concerning any rites which might have been employed then. There is, in fact, no sign that any of the medieval Irish writers who referred to it preserved a memory of them, and some evidence that they no longer understood the meaning of the name itself.[28]

The historical Feast of St. Brigid is much better attested than the feast of Imbolc, whatever it was. As with the case of the supposed triple-goddess Brigit, the Imbolc that Brigid's feast day is supposed to have been derived from is not even attested until centuries *after* her death. As Dr. Hutton says, it probably does date back to pre-Christian times, but other than its coincidental concurrence with Brigid's date of death, there is no other connection to the saint.

6. Similarities Between Brigid and Celtic Myth?

Alleged similarities between Brigid and Celtic myth are ubiquitous online, but they are always extremely vague. When we search for specific episodes in the life of Brigid that supposedly parallel anything from Celtic myth, we are left empty. This is obviously because nothing at all is known about the goddess Bríg upon whom Brigid is supposedly based.

On the continent, there are inscriptions mentioning a deity *Brigantia*, from the late Roman period. Nothing is known about her, however, or if she bears any similarity to the Irish Bríg.

---

[28] Ronald Hutton, *The Stations of the Sun: A History of the Ritual Year in Britain* (Oxford University Press, 1996), 134.

Part of the problem is that the old Celtic word *breo* simply means "high" or "powerful." *Brigantia* thus simply means "high one," "mighty one," or "powerful one." This makes discerning the identity of this deity a bit of a muddle; analogous to a situation where archaeologists in the distant future discovered English inscriptions to a being called "God-Almighty" and were uncertain if this phrase was a title or a proper name—or to ancient Canaan, where the etymology of the god Baal simply means "Lord," making it uncertain if this was a proper name or title. The morpheme *breo* and all its variants are extremely common throughout Indo-European languages; there are versions of it in Old German, Iberian, and even Sanskrit. It is as common in these tongues as the root *el* in Hebrew names, which also designates might, power, and divinity.

This has all taken us rather far afield from the main point, which is that so little is known about Bríg or Brigantia that no similarities to St. Brigid can even be posited let alone demonstrated.

Having addressed these six points, we shall conclude this essay by citing Dr. Clare Downham's assessment of the question in her scholarly tome, *Medieval Ireland.* After speaking about the foundation of Kildare, she says of Brigid:

> There is debate among scholars as to whether she was a real woman or a pagan goddess transmuted into a Christian saint. Nevertheless, evidence for a pre-Christian cult of Brigit in Kildare is lacking, and the earliest hagiography was written less than 150 years after her

supposed death: these details favour the view
that she was a real person.[29]

This last point is key: the *vitae* of the historical Brigid—along
with her tomb at Kildare and the community she founded—
all predate any reference to these pagan elements by
centuries. We do not know how old Cogitosus was when he
wrote his *vita*; if he was elderly at the time, then it is possible
he could have spoken with witnesses who personally knew
Brigid. Even if he was not, he certainly obtained his
information from secondary sources. It is ridiculous to
discount the testimony of Cogitosus—who had the
"extensive tradition" of Brigid's life at Kildare at his disposal
from the living memory of witnesses—in favor of a slipshod
theory cobbled together by Victorian speculators out of
fragmentary medieval references that post-date St. Brigid by
centuries.

---

[29] Clare Downham, *Medieval Ireland* (Cambridge University Press:
Cambridge, U.K., 2018), 121-122.

Printed in the USA
CPSIA information can be obtained
at www.ICGtesting.com
LVHW091009150324
774578LV00005B/76

9 781957 206073